The Power of God's Grace

(formerly entitled
Good News for Bad People)

The Power of God's Grace

by

Roy Hession

(formerly entitled
Good News for Bad People)

Rickfords Hill Publishing Ltd.

RICKFORDS HILL PUBLISHING LTD.
Perch Cottage, Halton Lane, Wendover. HP22 6AZ.
www.rhpbooks.co.uk

First Published 1989
Published by Rickfords Hill Publishing 2003
This edition 2008

ISBN: 978-1-905044-14-6

Typeset by Avocet Typeset, Chilton, Aylesbury, Buckinghamshire.

Cover design and print production for the publisher by Bookprint Creative Services, <www.bookprint.co.uk> Printed in Great Britain.

Dedicated to the Memory of

EVE JAMES

beloved wife of an English minister who chose the cassettes of my Bible Studies on which this book is based as her favourite listening and who played them to herself again and again. In her last illness she was listening to them yet once more, when the Lord called her to glory. By a significant coincidence she had not reached on this occasion the final theme of the tapes "Glorification for the Redeemed". She did not need to hear that final one again. She had entered the reality by our Lord Jesus Christ, and she is there with Him now.

The vile, the lost, He calls to them,
You trembling souls, appear!
The righteous in their own esteem
Have no acceptance here.

Approach, you poor, nor dare refuse
The banquet spread for you;
Dear Saviour, this is welcome news,
Then I may venture too.

If GUILT and SIN afford a plea,
And may obtain a place;
Surely the LORD will welcome me,
And I shall see His face.

William Cowper
1731–1800

Contents

Preface   ix

1   GOOD NEWS
     for bad people   1

2   JESUS
     for the sinner   13

3   RECONCILIATION
     for the enemy   31

4   GRACE
     for the undeserving   53

5   BLOOD
     for the remission of sin   71

6   FORGIVENESS
     for the guilty   93

7   CLEANSING
     for the defiled   113

8   JUSTIFICATION
     for the ungodly   125

9   REPENTANCE
     for sinner and saint   143

10   GLORIFICATION
     for the redeemed   157

Preface

The message and material for this book are based on five Bible Readings I gave some years ago on the subject of "Great Words of the Gospel" at a Christian Holiday Conference held annually at Southwold, Suffolk, England. Happily they were preserved on tape and were later typed verbatim. There the matter remained for several years with the material stored in my study. Latterly, the Lord put it on my heart to make a book of it so that it might be available for the blessing of the next generation.

However, there was a need for a more complete exposé of the whole message of grace which I have been seeking to proclaim ever since I was confonted with revival in 1947, as it came to these shores through the testimony and teaching of a team of missionaries and African leaders, who had met the Lord Jesus afresh in what is now known as the East Africa revival. Though I was a full-time evangelist, I was profoundly moved by this confrontation with living revival, as were many others, and I began a new walk with the Lord. As a result, I was given progressively a new concept of the gospel of the grace of God by means of which God accomplishes the revival of His church and the salvation of the lost. This book is the direct result of that new concept.

What was needed in this book was something more than a setting down word for word of what had been recorded on tape. These great truths have had to be researched again and again and entered personally into anew. They have also been amplified and instead of only five "great words" we now have ten. The studies, then, are not merely a repeat of what was said on those cassettes, but, I trust, a new creation.

There is another reason why it is important to have these precious things fully set out, because the phrase, "the message of grace", is often used (at least it is in the circles I move in) to indicate a ministry which proceeds along revival lines, either personal revival, or corporate revival. If it is used without its meaning being made clear, it becomes a chiché and ends by meaning nothing at all to the hearers. But the message of grace is no cliché; it is the message of the whole Bible, and wherever you look you will find it, in the Old Testament as well as in the New, and it all culminates in the Lord Jesus Himself: "We beheld His glory ... full of grace and truth." When it is seen that it is all for sinners, we bow in awe and penitence, and we find release.

Now a word about the title, "Good News for Bad People". I came across this definition of the gospel years ago in a little tract written by a beloved Bible teacher of a former generation, Montague Goodman. He did not make much of the phrase; it was slipped into a paragraph en passant, but it has stuck with me ever since and I have repeated it times without number, as those who have often heard me preach will testify. For me it exactly defines what the grace of our God is to sinners, and no other words could convey a better title for this book.

If the one who is reading these pages is a Christian of many years standing and well-instructed in the Bible, I beg of him not to think that he knows it all and that these gospel truths are milk for him, not meat. On every one of these great words of the gospel God has shed for me new light and given new insights that I never knew before revival came, although I was a preacher. They are the things by which I live right up to today, and apart from which I would be "dying on my feet".

I am writing for the professing Christian, as he is likely to be the first person to pick up this book, and its message is especially for him. Although its title, "Good News for Bad People", might make it appear to be solely an evangelistic book, the "bad people" of the title can very often be converted persons. I know from my own experience that such can often be lacking and out of touch with God. Such people need to know that God has got good news for them and that when the good news is embraced again, it will mean real revival for them and they will sing again as when they rejoiced in the day of their conversion. This book is really a handbook of revival theology. This revival must begin in the heart of the Christian – it will not end there, of course, but it must begin there. I would like to think he will therefore approach it with excitement and a spirit of expectancy.

Then, too, I am indeed writing for the lost. I like that term, lost; it is a biblical word and a tender one for those without Christ; if they are lost, Someone is looking for them. The truths in this book are the message by which such are found by Him. Though I have extended these gospel truths to cover the needs of believers, the good news is first for the lost ones.

Thirdly, I am bearing in mind all the time my brother preachers, ministers, evangelists and others – sisters, too – charged with passing on the message to others. As I share these rediscoveries of grace, I trust such will be helped and pollinated by what is here opened up, and set on fire to preach the good news as never before. They may discover that they have been giving only good advice, rather than good news. It could well be a theological revolution for some, though it will doubtless take time to work itself through to their places of utterance. It is one thing to know personal revival; it is another to have our whole thinking so reorientated as to be able to verbalise it clearly for others. This book, then, is for lost sinners, needy Christians, preachers, the latter being sometimes the neediest of all – I write as one myself.

I see yet another possibility in these chapters; it is that they might be used in group Bible studies. I have, therefore, arranged that the Bible references should not be left in the body of the text where they only confuse the eye, but put at the bottom of each page as footnotes where they can easily be spotted and quickly turned to by the reader. The version used throughout is the Authorised Version (known also as the King James Version), though I have adopted here and there words and phrases from other versions where I think they are especially helpful, but without detailing these small changes.

You would be advised not to attempt to read the whole book at a sitting, but rather to take a chapter or two at a time and give yourself space to digest the truth and apply it to your experience. But don't quit halfway through – some of the most explosive truths are in the latter half, especially the last chapter! – and do not allow the gaps between reading to be too long, otherwise you might forget what you have read.

As you proceed with this book I would urge upon you the prayer Jonah prayed when he found himself in the belly of the whale: "Then I said, I am cast out of Thy sight; yet I will look again toward Thy holy temple." What a situation he found himself in! Cast out, it seemed, from God's sight. He had only himself to blame for it. Yet in his extremity he said he would look again to God's holy temple, that place of which God had said in answer to Solomon's prayer, "I have chosen this place for Myself for a house of sacrifice." It was to be the place towards which Israel were to pray in their hour of calamity, when God would hear from heaven His dwelling place and hearing, forgive their sin and restore their cause. This is what Jonah did. As he lay entangled in the entrails of that whale, I imagine he must have said, "I don't know in which direction that house of sacrifice lies, I am so disorientated down here, but I'll take a chance and look again to where I think

God's holy temple is and trust I've got it right." The ancient promise still stood, the sacrifice offered in that house still availed, and God heard from heaven, forgave his sin, delivered him from the whale and sent him back again to Nineveh with astonishing results.

LOOK AGAIN

I would urge you in your own hour of need to look again – not to some new, or deeper, or more complicated formula for victory, but to the ancient place of sacrifice, Calvary's cross, and to that old gospel which you thought you knew so well, but which you have not been applying to the deeper needs of your life. Above all, look to Jesus, who is the heart and centre of it all.

> *"There is life for a look at the crucified one,*
> *There is life at this moment for thee".*

If you should say, "But I have looked already; I've been a Christian for years," then, brother, sister, look again. If you ever feel you have cause to say, "I'm cast out of Thy sight", remember that Jonah said, "Yet I will look again toward Thy holy temple."

I am aware that to give a book entitled "Good News for Bad People" to another whom you deem to be in special need because of some wrong doing might be embarrassing. It might imply that he needs it, while you, well, you do not, at least, not in the same degree. Be sure to tell him or her that you yourself are one of the "bad" – and that alone is why you qualify for the good news. Indeed, it might be that the giving of this book should always be accompanied by some such testimony.

ROY HESSION
England

"And the angel of the Lord said unto them, Fear not: for, behold I bring you good news of great joy which shall be to all people" (Luke 2:10).

"And when Jesus had opened the book, He found the place where it was written, The Spirit of the Lord is upon Me, because He hath anointed Me to preach good news to the poor" (Luke 4:17, 18).

1

GOOD NEWS
for bad people

The message which this book proclaims, Good News for bad people, is not a joke, nor even a snappy Christian title; it is serious theology, gospel theology. Indeed, I would call it revival theology, for I have been learning it ever since I was confronted with revival years ago. Within its five short words is compressed the whole message of revival, the message of grace. Finney, the great theologian and evangelist of the nineteenth century, said, "Revival always presupposes a declension[1]" and the very word "revival", beginning with the Latin prefix *re* meaning "again", says as much. It is God doing a work again in the hearts of those in whom there has been a spiritual declension. It is not a green valley getting greener, but a valley full of dry bones being made to stand up an exceeding great army;[2] it is not good Christians becoming better Christians, but those whose valley has become dead and full of bones being made to bring forth fruit again. It stands to reason that those who are the most ready to admit

---

[1] *Declension* means 'a deterioration'   [2] Ezekiel 37:1–14.

to declension will be amongst the first to partake of the blessing of revival.

With this in mind I want to take the words of this title very seriously, and give them a careful scrutiny, aspect by aspect. They will give us the clue to much else that we shall study together.

Good news

When the angel of the Lord appeared to the shepherds during the time of the nativity, he said, "Behold I bring you *good news* of great joy which shall be to all people".[3] Later at Nazareth, when Jesus had opened the Scriptures, He read, "The Spirit of the Lord is upon Me because He hath anointed Me to preach *good news* to the poor".[4] The coming of Jesus was to proclaim good news. This is the literal meaning of the word gospel.

That is what we ought to be hearing in our churches – good news. But we hear precious little of it. What usually passes for good news is all too often good advice. It is very good advice, sometimes quite scholarly good advice, and no one would doubt the sincerity or its orthodoxy – but it is still only good advice, with very little good news about it.

The weakness of good advice is that we ourselves are weak. What we have to say about good advice is what Paul had to say about the law, "It is weak through the flesh".[5] Excellent as it may be, we do not have the moral power to rise to it. In any case, it

---

[3]Luke 2:10.   [4]Luke 4:18.   [5]Romans 8:1

almost certainly comes too late; the things counselled against have already been done, and good advice at this stage is little more than shutting the stable door after the horse has bolted.

I remember when I was a boy about to go to boarding school, my widowed mother felt she must apprise me of the facts of life with regard to sex and give me due warnings. My father was dead and there was no one to do it but herself. She took me into a room, turned out the light to hide her embarrassment and told me. She gave me, bless her heart, splendid advice that day, but it was too late.

When Jesus comes to us He does not come with good advice, but with good news. He does not say, "Don't do this, and don't do that", but He says, "You've done them already, but I come to you with good news". What news?

"The joyful news of sins forgiven,
Of hell subdued and peace with heaven".

Those two lines of a famous hymn are but the merest summary of the good news. The rest of these studies of the Great Words of the Gospel will be an exploration of the fulness of that good news, which I trust will almost take your breath away. Even when the worst has come to the worst, such is the extent of grace, Jesus has provided for everything in advance and He says to you, "Be of good cheer, your sins be forgiven you".[6] Your sins and any calamities that

---

[6]Matthew 9:2.

may fall upon you may take you by surprise; they never take Him so; He has anticipated them all and He always has good news for you.

All this for bad people

The fact that a person's track record hardly bears inspection, that there is little that they can point to that is to their credit, that there is many a blot on their escutcheon makes no difference to the favour of God toward them. They are still loved as sinners and given every opportunity and encouragement to repent. A favourite verse with many of us in the book of Revelation is, "Unto Him that loved us and washed us from our sins in His own blood".[7] It does not say He washed us from our sins and then loved us, but He loved us as we were and then washed us. In other words, He came with good news for bad people.

This is tremendous. It is the best definition that could be devised for that strange, wondrous quality in the Godhead which is called grace, the undeserved favour of God. There is a whole chapter on this subject, but suffice it to say now that if we had all the theological professors in the world together, we could not define what grace is more fully than the title, "Good News for bad people". One would expect that if God had good news to give it would be for good people. To be told, however, that God has good news for bad

---

[7]Revelation 1:5.

people is the very reverse of what we would expect and seems to outrage our sense of moral values. Yet this is the gospel that Jesus came into the world to bring. Nothing less than this is the meaning of this word, grace.

It would not be good news if it were only for the good, for in God's sight none of us is in that category – "there is none that doeth good, no not one."[8] But the good news is custom-made for sinners, and that being the case, all of us qualify, "for there is no difference, for all have sinned".[9] Once sin comes into a life, God is concerned with only one thing – recovery. He is not interested in inquests; it is recovery He is after. This makes His good news even better news.

Even for Christians

This Good News for bad people still holds good, even when the bad people happen to be *converted. I* know that to speak of converted persons being "bad" will sound strange to some, but the fact is that even people who know Christ as their Saviour can do the wrong thing, can react in the wrong way, can get into a wrong relationship with others and find themselves in tangled circumstances through their own fault. If that is not being "bad", what is? Even for them God has good news.

When Christians fail they are sometimes thrown into a special form of despair, when they remember their lapses have been against the backdrop of the

---

[8]Romans 3:12.   [9]Romans 3:22, 23.

personal love of Christ for them. They must be persuaded that recovery is possible; that it is never too late to repent, that no situation is too far gone for grace. Not only must they see that God has made provision for their recovery, but it is essential they should avail themselves of it, from the largest matters right down to the smallest. They need to be assured that the blood of Christ provides complete recovery and there is no cause for further despair. I remind them that when David had found his way back to God after his grievous fall, he not only said, 'Blessed is the man whose iniquities are forgiven and whose sins are covered", but he added, "and to whom the Lord will not impute sin"[1] that is, to whom not one spot of blame attaches. If that were not enough, he adds further, "and in whose spirit there is no guile."[2] That is, "I'm not hiding anything now"!

Honest admission

All this is on the implied condition that the bad confess they are bad, for how can I receive good news for bad persons unless I confess I am one of them myself? If your heart gets touched by this good news, you would not want to do otherwise. Or would you? You are in need of even greater help from God if you hope to receive the good news while still retaining duplicity in your heart.

It is this implied condition that puts teeth into the message of grace, and leads us to judge sin in

---

[1]Psalm 32:1.   [2]Psalm 32:2.

ourselves. Very often an implied condition is much more compelling than a clearly stated one. It is left to you to do what you think is right and appropriate in view of the boon that is proffered you, "be of good cheer, your sins are forgiven." And you find yourself strangely willing. More, you have the fellowship and Christian affection of others who are also enjoying the good news for the bad, because each can testify that they qualify as such themselves. Is it not ironic that the very quality (being sinners), that we thought would exclude us, actually gives us in the reverse the sense of belonging?

Candidate for grace

This short spiritual journey leads us to the happy conclusion that being willing to take the sinner's place makes us *candidates for the grace of God.* When we get to the chapter on grace, the undeserved favour of God, we shall see more how our very acknowledgement of being wrong makes us candidates for grace. The grace of God is not for those who are right, but only for those who are wrong. By its very nature it no longer has to find in me the procuring cause to draw forth the needed blessing. It would not be grace if that were necessary. Merely to take the sinner's place (I call that being broken) is enough to give me all the qualification I need. I am not a candidate for grace if I claim to be in the right; only when I confess I am in the wrong. What an inducement, then, to take that blessed place and have all as grace!

A recent re-reading of the eighteenth century revival in the days of the Wesleys has given me new light on this call to repentance. Charles Wesley had been converted and had found peace with God somewhat before his brother John did; he certainly moved forward at the beginning faster and with greater enthusiasm and assurance. Immediately he began to testify to all and sundry and spoke of his new discovery of grace for sinners in every pulpit that was open to him. He says of one of his meetings in a religious society, "I urged upon each my usual question, 'Do you deserve to be damned?' Mrs Platt, with the utmost vehemence cried out, 'Yes, I do! I do!'" We are not told in his journal who this Platt was or what happened further, but I am sure she was immediately assured by Wesley that she now qualified by that very acknowledgement for the good news, and she began to rejoice in the Lord Jesus.

There, then, is the beginning of our theme of grace drawn deep from God's word – good news for bad people, even when the bad happen to be converted, and all on the simple condition that they honestly acknowledge their badness, which acknowledgement makes them candidates as never before for the grace of God and all the blessings of salvation and/or revival.

What a paradox it all is! In the school of grace everything is the other way round from what one would expect; the top is at the bottom and the back is at the front. That being so, it should not be too surprising to find God proclaiming good news for bad people. This way lies the revival of the church.

Three classes

I would like to make a very personal application to the reader. I want to suggest that most people can be divided into three classes and it might be helpful if you try to assess which class you fall into. Such a self-assessment might be the beginning of a new life.

The first class comprises the *bad who do not know they are bad.* The great majority of us, whether we are in the churches or out of them, do not regard ourselves as bad. Whatever our life-style or conduct, we have found some way to justify ourselves. Man is a moral being and could not live with himself if he saw himself as wholly bad. Therefore self-justification is a natural part of everybody's life. Man has lied to himself about himself for so long that he has ultimately come to believe his own lie, and he is quite sincere in believing that he is not intrinsically bad. The fact that he may be religious only reinforces his good opinion of himself. That is where God has to begin with every man. And He has to find ways and means of introducing that man to himself and convincing him that the deepest, truest thing about him is that he is a sinner. How He does this will vary.

In the case of the prophet Isaiah, He did it by giving him a vision of the seraphim surrounding the throne of God in worship, but covering their faces and their feet before the One who sat upon that throne. Isaiah saw creatures greater in power and might than ever he could be, yet their supreme concern was to hide self before God. In the light of that he saw that his supreme concern had all along been to display self. He realised that "be seen, be known, be heard", had been the order of the day for him. It was only when he saw the seraphim hiding themselves that he uttered his brokenhearted prayer of confession; "Then said I, Woe is me! for I am undone; because I am a man of unclean lips … for mine eyes have seen the King, the Lord of Hosts".[3]

With others of us He may have different ways of showing us what we are. Till then we go on blissfully ignorant of the truth about ourselves. The fact that we cannot see anything wrong, or any cause for alarm, does not mean there is nothing wrong. It may simply mean that we are blind. This may well necessitate our first confession to be, "Lord, forgive me for my blindness".

The second class is comprised of *bad people who are trying to be good.* Sincere as they may be, it is vain for such people to hope that it is going to improve their relationship with God, or that it will greatly change their personal experience. The Bible not only teaches they will not become good enough for heaven, but suggests that they will have Paul's experience of trying to be good; "the good that I would I do not, and the evil that I would not that I do";[4] and they will end up by saying with him, "Oh wretched man that I am, who will deliver me?"[5]

If that is not our experience, it is simply because we are not trying hard enough! We will never know that trying is not the way to peace until we have

---

[3]Isaiah 6:1–5.   [4]Romans 7:19.   [5]Romans 7:24.

tried trying, really tried. Only then will we know that we will never make it. For the bad to try to be good is the surest way for them to miss heaven.

Jesus, the end of trying

The third class is composed of the group in whom the Holy Spirit has done a melting work, *the bad humbly confessing to God that they are bad* and not pleading any extenuating circumstances. As far as they are concerned there is only one person at the bar before God and that is themselves. When they take that stand they immediately become candidates for the good news that Jesus has for them and for the grace that is greater than all their sin. For them Jesus is the end of trying, and the beginning of finding. They run to Him with all their lack and He, on His part, becomes all they need. He turns on the electricity, so to speak. Some people call it being born again; others who have already been born again, but have left their first love,[6] call it revival.

---

[6]Revelation 2:4.

"And thou shalt call His Name Jesus: for He it is that shall save His people from their sins" (Matthew 1:21).

"A virgin shall conceive, and bear a Son and shall call His Name Immanuel" (Isaiah 7:14).

"It pleased the Father that in Him should all fulness dwell" (Colossians 1:19).

2

JESUS
for the sinner

Of the great words of the Gospel, Jesus is the greatest of them all. In the New Testament He is called the Word. "In the beginning was the Word, and the Word was with God, and the Word was God."[1] As the word is son of the thought and exactly expresses it, so is Jesus the Son of God and exactly expresses Him. "He is the brightness of His glory and the express image of His Person."[2] The God who was inaudible, invisible and intangible was expressed in Jesus and in Him became audible, visible and even tangible, and the apostles left the record of it for us. "That which we have heard, which we have seen with our eyes, which we have looked upon and our hands have handled of the Word of life … declare we unto you."[3]

The good news is that this great and glorious Jesus is all for the sinner. He was made flesh for the sinner, He died for the sinner, He rose again for the sinner, and He is at this moment appearing in the presence of God for the sinner. Jesus belongs to him

---

[1]John 1:1.   [2]Hebrews 1:3.   [3]1 John 1:1.

if only by the sinner's sins, for it was because of them that He came. These sins, if duly acknowledged and repented of, become a sinner's very qualification for Jesus.

What's in a name?

This extraordinary grace is revealed by the special name that was given Him by divine appointment. Shakespeare asked, "What's in a name? That which we call a rose by any other name would smell as sweet." Not so in Scripture where names are treated seriously. In Scripture the name often describes the character and destiny of the one to whom it is given and the naming of a child often had a prophetic quality. That was certainly true of Jesus. Christ is His title, meaning Messiah, but there are two names given to Him in the Bible.

First, that which the angel revealed to Joseph, husband of Mary, "Fear not to take unto thee Mary thy wife: for that which is conceived in her is of the Holy Spirit. And she shall bring forth a Son, and thou shalt call His Name Jesus."[4] JE is an abbreviation of Jehovah, the Name revealed to Moses at the burning bush, meaning, I AM; and SUS is an abbreviation of another Hebrew word meaning saviour, thus making the name of JESUS to mean JEHOVAH SAVIOUR. Immediately there follows a sentence giving the reason for that name, an exposition of it, "for He it is that shall save His people from their sins". Jesus is

---

[4]Matthew 1:20, 21.

the same Jehovah, who has been seen in so many different capacities in the Old Testament, and is now seen in the New Testament in His capacity as saviour from sin. Saviour is His name because saving His people from their sins is His business, His calling. It is not said, "He shall reward His people for their righteousness," nor is it promised that "He shall save them from becoming sinners", but "He shall save His people from their sins", the sins that are already there. Note, He will not only save the lost from their sins, but His people. Apparently His people have their sins too, and His saving includes them also. By the very name He bears He is a specialist in saving His people from their sins.

If, however, they will not have it that they have any sins worth speaking about and are therefore unwilling to repent, their fancied righteousness only has the effect of wiping out the name of Jesus as Saviour, as far as their experience is concerned. But if you, as one of them, do know that you have sins and can name them only too easily and, indeed, have your back to the wall in your struggle against some of them, then Jesus by the very name given Him is the saviour you need. Go to Him and say, "Oh Lord Jesus, be Jesus to me; be a true Jesus in my experience." He will not fail to fulfil His own name and show His power in you. Only confess to Him your sin and He will save you from it.

C.H. Spurgeon in a glorious sermon on this text, "He shall save His people from their sins" says,

"Notice the very gracious, but startling fact that our Lord's connection with His people lies in the direction of their sins … The first link between my soul and Christ is not my goodness, but my badness; not my merit, but my misery; not my standing, but my falling; not my riches, but my need. He comes to visit His people, yet not to admire their beauties, but to remove their deformities; not to reward their virtues, but to forgive their sins." Be encouraged, therefore, really to lay hold by faith on such a One with such a name with regard to your personal need. You have a personal Saviour for your personal sin.

His second name

The same passage goes on to give Him a second name. "Now all this was done that it might be fulfilled which was spoken of the Lord by the prophet, 'Behold, a virgin shall be with child and shall bring forth a son and they shall call His name Emmanuel.'"[5] This is a quotation of a well-known virgin prophecy in the Old Testament. Every Hebrew would know the meaning of Emmanuel in his language. But Matthew had Gentiles in mind who would not know Hebrew and so he gives the translation for their benefit, "which is being interpreted, 'God with us.'"

This is what God had always wanted – to dwell with the man whom He had created and not be a

[5]Matthew 1:22, 23.

God afar off. When He instructed Moses to erect the tabernacle in the wilderness, He said,"Speak unto the Children of Israel that they bring Me an offering … and let them make Me a sanctuary that I may dwell among them."[6] That tabernacle in the wilderness was a symbol of God's age-long desire to dwell with man and was prophetic that He would indeed do so one day.

This is what man has always wanted, too, as expressed in the words of Job, "Oh that I knew where I might find Him."[7] He wanted a God near at hand, so that there would be no need for man to try to ascend into heaven to bring Him down, or to descend into the deep to bring Him up. Isaiah in his prophecy about the virgin-born Son said that Jehovah was going to be just that, and not in symbolic form, but in actual fact. In the Son that the virgin was to bear God was going to dwell with man and therefore His Name was to be Emmanuel, God with us, available to us on our level. This, then, is Jesus.

There is no need for us to try to climb higher by self-improvement, that is to bring Him down, for He has already come down; or to descend by some forced humility into the depths, that is to bring Him up, for He has already come up. He is God available to you as you are and where you are, not only physically, but morally. Jesus really is the saviour of the sinner as a sinner, what someone has called, "the message of street-level grace". This is good news

---

[6]Exodus 25:2, 8.   [7]Job 23:3.

indeed for those of us who have never been able to make it up or down.

I have been interested in reading George Whitefield's journals to see that Emmanuel was his favourite name for Jesus. He often refers to Jesus as his Emmanuel. I can only infer that the message of street-level grace had got hold of him in his experience, and we, too, out of many experiences of this grace can gratefully sing,

> *Emmanuel, Emmanuel,*
> *His Name is called Emmanuel,*
> *God with us, brought down to us,*
> *He's rightly called Emmanuel.*

The close proximity in Matthew's Gospel of these two names, Jesus and Emmanuel, makes the latter almost a synonym of the former. Jesus not only saves His people from their sins but is available to them as they are without one plea, except their need on their part and His blood on His part. He is a specialist in the realm of sin, neither shocked nor defeated by it, for He has in Himself the complete answer, "that wonderful redemption, God's remedy for sin". He is not famous for the number of good Christians He pats on the back – none of us is good enough for that – but for the sinners He saves, the transgressions He forgives, the messes He clears up, the relationships He heals, and the fulness of His life which He pours into otherwise empty hearts. Great as is the power of Jesus seen in creation ("all things were made by Him, and without Him was not anything made that was made")[8], His power in the realm of grace is far, far greater. He not only forgives sin, but makes the marred vessel into another vessel, as seems good to the Potter to make it.[9]

All fulness in Jesus

There is perhaps no part of Scripture that gives a more complete picture of the fulness of Jesus and His availability to the believer in his need than does Paul's epistle to the Colossians.

In chapter one he writes, "It pleased the Father that in Him all fulness should dwell."[1] The word translated "fulness" is that which fills, or completes what is lacking. In other words, this verse declares that the full provision for what is lacking in the experience of the Christian has been caused to dwell for him in Christ – peace, power, joy, victory, needed spiritual abilities, and much else. How much fulness does it say has been put there? All fulness; I do not need to go outside of Christ for anything. In other words, God has put it all where sinners, flops and failed saints like I am can get it, in Christ Jesus. This is truly good news.

It is a mistake, therefore, to seek any experience of blessing or spiritual gifts separate from and in addition to Jesus Christ. God has already put everything in Him. This is why we sometimes seek in vain; He Himself is all we need, and all that is necessary is the

---

[8]John 1:3.   [9]Jeremiah 18:4.   [1]Colossians 1:19.

simple confession to Him of whatever matter we are
lacking. Do nothing to hide or excuse that lack, and
certainly do not strive with your own efforts to meet
it, but simply confess it. Emptiness is the way to
fulness. This is what I call coming by the back door,
the beggar's door. Then our faith can sing its new
experience of grace:

> *Jesus Christ is made to me,*
>   *All I need, all I need;*
> *He alone is all my plea,*
>   *He is all I need.*
> *Wisdom, righteousness and power,*
>   *Holiness this very hour.*
> *My redemption* full *and sure.*
>   *He is all I need.*

Christ available to me

Paul goes on to speak of, "the mystery which hath
been hid from ages and from generations, but is now
made manifest to His saints: to whom God would
make known what is the riches of the glory of this
mystery among the Gentiles, which is *Christ in you,
the hope of glory*".[2] We shall not understand this apart
from its context. What Paul is referring to here is the
fact that the believing Gentiles are included on equal
terms with the believing Jews in the Body of Christ,
a theme which is stated even more fully in the
epistle to the Ephesians. In the Colossian epistle he

---

[2]Colossians 1:26, 27.

is speaking to the believing Gentiles and he says for their encouragement, "To whom God would make known what is the riches of the glory of this mystery (better translated, secret, that is something not before revealed), which is Christ in you, the hope of glory."

Here is a secret not revealed in the Old Testament, nor even in the four gospels. It was a special revelation entrusted to Paul, so much so that he could call himself the "Apostle to the Gentiles". Till then the Gentiles were considered "aliens from the commonwealth of Israel and strangers from the covenants of promise". Israel considered them so and the Gentiles thought the same about themselves. But here is a secret now revealed which had been "kept secret since the world began", totally without precedent and astonishing to both Jew and Gentile.

What was the secret? "Christ in you, the hope of glory". Most of us have taken that to refer to the indwelling of Jesus Christ in every believer. But the margin of the King James Version gives an alternative reading for the words "in you"; it says "Or, among you". This means that the word "in" can equally well be translated "among"; it depends on the context as to which is right and there is little doubt that the context favours the word "among". This makes the phrase, "Christ among you, (that is, available to you), is your hope of glory". Who are the "you"? The Gentiles, of course. This exactly fits in with the whole context of the passage and means that the secret never before revealed was that Christ, the Messiah, born of Israel, was available also to the unprivileged Gentiles as their sure and certain hope of glory, just as certainly as to believers in Israel.

This passage, then, is not speaking of the indwelling of Christ (that is taught in many other Scriptures), but of the availability of God's Messiah to the Gentiles, who normally had no qualification to be included. A Gentile might be qualified if he had proslytised and been circumcised and become a Jew by adoption. But here Jesus is seen to be available to the Gentiles as Gentiles, whether they were circumcised or not, and not only the Gentiles in that narrow sense of the word, but any of us today who consider ourselves unqualified for blessing and fellowship, either because of our background, or lack of education, or simply because of a poor spiritual track record. To such Jesus is available as they are, as sinners, and all apart from works. You can do works if you like, but they will not improve your chances one iota. Far, far better to confess your lack of them for in so doing you become one of those sinners to whom Jesus is available on street level as their sure and certain hope of glory.

Those last words are important – hope of glory. The word "hope" seems to imply an element of doubt, but not so the Greek word translated hope. There is nothing doubtful about that. It means a confident assurance, and that of going to glory when our life on earth ends. We will be more happy there, but not more secure, nor more sure than we can be now, for the promise of God who cannot lie ensures our eternal salvation. Jesus is our certain hope of glory. He is not only that to us, but our hope (our confident assurance) of everything else; our hope of peace, our hope of victory, and our hope of revival.

Complete in Him

Paul also tells the Colossian Christians "in Him dwelleth all the fulness of the Godhead bodily; and *ye are complete in Him*."[2] In coming to Jesus as I am in all honesty about my condition, I am not only received by Him, but made complete in Him. As a hymn says, "I nothing lack if I am His, and He is mine for ever". I do not need anything more than Jesus. It is a mistake for a Christian to think that he would be complete if only he had more power, or various gifts, or if his group were seeing signs and wonders. These things may well be experienced by some, but the intense seeking for them as something extra may well lead a person away from Jesus and away from grace and away from repentance. If, on the other hand, we avail ourselves of Him and His blood as the sinners we are, we are complete in Him. If we are still conscious of dryness and spiritual coldness, we do not need to seek something extra and unusual, but simply to be more open to God's conviction of sin and to be more specific in repentance and to be more confident in the power of His blood to cleanse from sin and thus go deeper into

---

[2]Colossians 2:9, 10.

Him in whom all fulness dwells – the One in whom we are complete.

"Be not moved away"

It was because some of the Colossians were being tempted to seek something extra that he says, "Be not moved away from the hope of the gospel."[3] He would not have said that unless they were in danger of doing it. In actual fact they had already done it and that in at least four matters which he details in the second chapter – four emphases which had come in and taken Jesus' place in the centre. We need not look at them in detail because there has always been a tendency for the church to deviate from having Christ in the centre. If it is not one thing, it will be another. In the Ephesian epistle you find Paul battling with the problem again; "Be no more children carried about with every wind of doctrine … but grow up into Christ in all things."[4] When Christians get taken up with the latest fad or doctrine or emphasis or method and put that in the centre, they are like babies playing with toys, who need to grow up. It is not a sign of advanced spirituality, but rather of immaturity.

> *When different winds of doctrine blow,*
> *Then set their sails who will,*
> *But as for me, content I go*
> *To Calvary's lonely hill.*

---

[3]Colossians 1:23.   [4]Ephesians 4:14, 15.

Let others cry for greater power
And marvellous gifts declare,
But all I ask is every hour
My Christ to know, my Christ to share.

Let others tell of mighty signs
And miracles they've seen,
But keep me, Lord, in light that shines
And shows where I'm unclean.

May grace be given to bring the sin,
Contrite to Calvary,
My only goal be Christ to win,
My only good be He.

From Calvary there flows God's love,
The love of Christ to me;
No wind of doctrine shall remove
Me from that fruitful tree.

I need not fear, I have within
The friendly Paraclete,
He shows me Christ, He shows me sin,
He shows the Mercy Seat.

So, worthy Lamb, I join the song
That the redeemed will sing,
A member of that blood-washed throng
Who gather round their King.

Dr Kenneth Moynagh

Fountain or cistern?

Because this deviating is so prevalent, it is possible that the person reading this book has been doing exactly this, albeit unwittingly. I therefore bring here the message that Jeremiah brought to Israel, which is as pertinent for us today as it was for them in their day.

Said he, "The word of the Lord came to me, saying … My people have committed two evils; they have forsaken Me, the fountain of living waters, and hewed them out cisterns, broken cisterns that can hold no water. "[5] The first evil He charges them with is one against Himself, which has hurt and saddened Him; "they have forsaken Me the fountain of living waters." Jesus describes Himself as the fountain of living waters. He said to the woman of Samaria, "The water that I shall give you shall become in you a spring of water welling up unto eternal life."[6] When a Christian puts a pet emphasis or formula, or anything else in the centre he is guilty of forsaking Jesus as the fountain of living waters. I know because I have done it myself. At all costs, he must see what he has done, as I had to.

The second evil He charges them with is that for the fountain they have substituted a cistern of their own making.

In forsaking the fountain for the cistern they have exchanged that which was the source of water for that which at best could only store it. As the farmer

---

[5]Jeremiah 2:13.   [6]John 4:14.

saw that impressive cistern or reservoir, which he had created full of water collected from recent rainfalls, he felt himself much safer than when he only had that modest-looking spring to depend on. But it was only a store of water, and not the source of it. Jesus alone is the source; we cannot have both as objects of trust.

They have also forsaken that which was theirs gratuitously and without effort for that which has cost them much effort and toil. They had "*hewed them out cisterns*". All substitutes for Christ involve self-effort, striving and works. They can sometimes almost kill us when all the time the supply of the Spirit was ours "without money and without price" in Jesus Christ. Had we but known it, the supply of the Spirit was never to be received as the reward of our faithfulness, but simply and only as God's gift for our acknowledged weaknesses.

Lastly, they forsook that which never failed them in the past for a cistern that was soon broken and therefore could hold no water. Although that spring did not look very spectacular, the farmer never found it to fail, not even in drought. But the cistern soon developed a fissure and was one long disappointment.

> *I tried the broken cisterns, Lord,*
> *But, ah, the waters failed,*
> *E'en as I stooped to drink they fled,*
> *And mocked me as I wailed.*

What could have induced you to make such a tragic

exchange? Could it be that some debris of sin had fallen into the mouth of the spring and choked it and therefore you had to try something else? That something else could have been part of what D.R. Davies used to call, "The art of dodging repentance". Was this the philosophy that all unsuspected lay behind that change of stance on your part?

All is not lost if you will learn from the ruins of the broken cisterns. Remember from whence thou art fallen and repent. Return to the fountain and learn to live there.

> *Now none but Christ can satisfy,*
> *None other name for me;*
> *There's love and life and lasting joy,*
> *Lord Jesus, found in Thee.*

"All things are of God, who hath reconciled us to Himself by Jesus Christ, and hath given unto us the ministry of reconciliation, to wit that God was in Christ, reconciling the world unto Himself, not imputing their trespasses unto them; and hath committed unto us the word of reconciliation. Now then we are ambassadors for Christ, as though God did beseech you by us; 'We pray you in Christ's stead, be ye reconciled to God, for He hath made Him to be sin for us, who knew no sin: that we might be made the righteousness of God in Him'" (2 Corinthians 5:18–21).

"For when we were yet without strength, in due time, Christ died for the ungodly. For scarcely for a righteous man will one die: yet peradventure for a good man some would even dare to die. But God commendeth His love toward us in that while we were yet sinners, Christ died for us. Much more, then, being justified by His blood, we shall be saved from wrath through Him. For if, when we were enemies, we were reconciled to God by the death of His Son, much more, being reconciled, we shall be saved by His life. And not only so, but we also joy in God through our Lord Jesus Christ, by whom we have received the reconciliation" (Romans 5:6–11).

3

RECONCILIATION
for the enemy

Reconciliation is surely the greatest and most magnanimous of the acts of God on behalf of man. The New Testament tells us that "when we were His enemies, we were reconciled to God by the death of His Son." He told us to love our enemies. He certainly did it Himself, and in doing it He saved us from ruin.

As normally understood, reconciliation means an ending of enmity and the making of peace and friendship between persons previously opposed. This is not merely a theological word, but is used in everyday secular situations. A father and his grown son may be at odds with one another, and we say they need to be reconciled. We use the same word if a bad relationship is developing between a man and his wife, which could lead to marital breakdown – they need to be reconciled. There may be two opposing groups of people, and we say they need to be reconciled. What a beautiful sight it is whenever we see it happen! And so I could go on quoting situations where there is need for reconciliation.

But there is one area, one relationship, where

reconciliation is more essential than any other; it is the area of man's relationship with God. You will see from the passage at the start of this chapter that the great call of the gospel is, "Be ye reconciled to God".[1] You may need to be reconciled to this person or that person, but before all else you need to be reconciled to God. Failure here is the basic cause of most of our other bad relationships which only enforce our need to be reconciled to God. This word is used with exactly the same meaning as in secular situations. If you know what it means for a man to need to be reconciled to another man, then you know what the word means when we talk about man needing to be reconciled to God.

Reconciliation with God is, however, not something that we do, though we have a response to make, but rather something that He achieves for us. This work of grace, and it is indeed a grace, has as its object the most undeserving of all people, those who have become the enemies of God. That something good should be done for enemies is astonishing, amazing grace indeed! God has taken action to reconcile men to Himself, so that His enemies can become His friends and loving servants.

There is no word that has more Gospel, that is, "Good News for bad people", compressed into it than this word. Indeed that great era of evangelism, the Moody era in the 19th century, was permeated through and through with this great truth of reconciliation with God. We can tell it not only from the

---

[1] 2 Corinthians 5:20.

sermons the evangelists of those days preached, but from the songs and hymns that Sankey and others bequeathed to us:

> *Earnestly, tenderly, Jesus is calling,*
> *Calling, O sinner, come home.*

You say, "There is something about the hymns of those days, what is it? – they are so moving, melting and compelling; they linger with us to this day." The answer is that they are almost all expressing the great truth that, "God was in Christ reconciling the world unto Himself, not imputing unto them their trespasses,"[2] and they all utter the earnest call, "We pray you in Christ's stead, be ye reconciled to God."

Whether or not those are the hymn tunes for today, the truth they express certainly is and we need a great tribe of men and women to be raised up as ambassadors for Christ to utter the call loud and clear to a world at war with God, "Be ye reconciled to God."

At enmity with God

When a person is first confronted with, "Be ye reconciled to God", it must be quite a shock, as for instance, a woman quietly minding her own business, "be thou reconciled to God"; or a man working 9 to 5, coming back each day to his home and garden

---

[2] 2 Corinthians 5:19.

and going to church each Sunday, "be thou reconciled to God"; or a group of young people enjoying
themselves, "be ye reconciled to God." Such a
person, or persons might say, "Be reconciled to God?
That implies that I'm at enmity with God, or at odds
with Him over something, or am taking the stance of
an enemy of the gospel. But I am quite unaware that
I have any such attitude! I quite approve of religion
and have nothing against it – for others."

The words "be reconciled to God" do imply all
that. This is what the Bible says, that we are enemies
of God and reconciliation with God is what is
needed, or we face total disaster.

In the verses from Romans chapter five set out
at the beginning of this chapter, man is shown in
a fourfold light. In verse 6 he is said to be *without
strength*, "while we were yet without strength",
that is, helpless to extricate himself from the situation of loss into which he has got himself. In the
same verse he is said to be *ungodly*, "Christ died
for the ungodly." In verse 8 he is seen as a sinner,
"while we were yet sinners" and in verse 10 he is
said to be an *enemy*, "when we were enemies". As
to his situation, he is without strength, that is,
helpless. As to his character, he is ungodly. As to
his condition, he is a sinner; and as to his attitude,
and this is the most important point just now and
the one I want to focus on, he is an enemy. Actions
are, of course, important. But far more important
is the attitude that lies behind the actions. To be
without strength, and ungoldly, and a sinner, is
bad, but it is worse, far worse, to be an enemy; it

beggars imagination! An enemy of God!

It does not mean that God is your enemy, but rather you are His enemy. It is not that He is against you, but rather that you are against Him. Not for one moment has God been your enemy, no matter how much you may have provoked Him. He loves you as much when you are wrong as when you are right. What it does mean is that in spite of all the goodness of God to you, you are at enmity with Him. That enmity exists in your mind, rather than in His. The plain teaching of Scripture is that by nature you and I are "alienated and enemies in our minds by wicked works."[3]

Sooner or later this will be apparent to you and to others who watch you when you turn down out of hand a godward course of some sort in favour of a more disreputable path. It is a part of our fallen human nature so to do. The Bible says, "the carnal mind is enmity against God".[4] The word "carnal" is the adjective of the noun "the flesh", that is, fallen human nature. The word "mind" means disposition. So this verse reads, "the disposition of the flesh is enmity against God". For good measure it goes on to say, "it is not subject to the law of God, neither indeed can be."

Inasmuch then as your greatest happiness both in time and in eternity is to be found in fellowship with God, your most urgent need is to be reconciled to Him. On His part He will be satisfied with nothing else and has taken the most extravagant action to

---

[3] Colossians 1:21.   [4] Romans 8:7.

achieve it for you. The amazing grace is that He has done it all while you are still an enemy! It says so in black and white: "when we were enemies we were reconciled to God by the death of His Son."

How the enmity began

Before we consider how God has achieved this reconciliation, we need to understand the way in which the great rift between man and God occurred in the first place and how the enmity toward Him has grown since. It began in the Garden of Eden, with man disobeying God's express command, that whereas he could eat of every tree of the garden, there was one tree of which he must not eat.[5] I suppose the reason why there was that prohibition was to prove to man that he was walking in obedience to God, for if there had been no prohibition how could it be known whether he was obeying or not? It was, however, the easiest of prohibitions; he had so many other trees of which to eat; it was only one he was to refrain from; he was not likely to go hungry. But just one thing prohibited is enough to make us want to do it and Satan worked on that.

C.S. Lewis in *Voyage to Venus*, his fantasy novel so full of spiritual meaning, tells us how the "fall" was narrowly averted on Venus. Dr Ransom on his splash-down in Venus finds that the only two people there are a couple in unfallen relationship to God, living on floating islands of large tropical

---

[5]Genesis 3:3.

vegetation in idyllic surroundings. They tell Dr Ransom that they are allowed to visit the fixed lands as they wish, but God has said they must never sleep the night there. That was the one prohibition. It was to get them to do just that and thus assert their independence of God that the person characterising Satan in the story uses every effort and philosophical argument. His attempt, however, was thwarted. But not, alas, in the real history in the Garden of Eden. Under the instigation of Satan, our first father and mother took of the forbidden fruit and committed the first sin and as a result acquired for the first time a guilty conscience toward God. That guilty conscience immediately made them feel that God was against them, shown by the fact that, when they heard His sound in the garden, they hid themselves from His presence among the trees. If asked why they were hiding, they would doubtless have answered, "Because now He is against us. He is furious with us because we have broken His commandment. Listen to Him calling, Adam, where art thou?'" The logic of their guilty conscience could come to no other conclusion.

The fact that they thought God was against them made them turn against Him. So has it been with all their descendants. A guilty conscience, and we all have that until we are cleansed of it, makes us feel that God is against us and disapproving of us. This in turn hardens us and puts us against Him and we act out our hostility by defying His moral laws and going our own way. That makes us quite sure He is the more against us because of the way we are living. That only hardens us and puts us the more against Him.

So the wretched spiral of enmity continues, until every overture of God to man is suspected of being the approach of an enemy masking unfriendly intentions. This is especially seen in a man's attitude to earnest Christians who might want to influence him for God. He watches them, suspects them, and avoids them. He is sure they are going to talk to him about his soul and they want to rob him of his little bit of happiness and independence. Isn't it extraordinary that in talking to such men away from God we have to be so careful lest we "put them off", as it is called? We are warned by those who are concerned for them, "Do be careful – he is so easily put off." That is strange – he would not be so easily put off if I merely had to announce to him the news that a relative of his had left him a fortune! But it is not strange – he is at enmity with God and is suspicious of what He is up to, because he feels, subconsciously or consciously, that God is against him.

More than that, when adversity or trouble comes, he will more than likely interpret it as God punishing him for his sins: I knew of a woman dying of cancer who said that God was punishing her for her secret unfaithfulness to her husband. Little inducement there for her to flee to God for refuge, while she thought that He was against her.

I care not how outwardly pious a person may be – every man is at enmity with God by nature, and this is the inner story of that enmity, with appropriate variations according to circumstances. The attitude lingers on even in the best.

God not against the sinner

All the time God is not against us. The imagined hostility on the part of God exists only in the mind of the sinner because of his guilty conscience. Not all the accumulated sins of the world have been able to put God against man for a moment. When God came down the garden asking, "Adam, where art thou?"[6] that was not the voice of a policeman looking for a criminal; it was the voice of a father who had lost a son and was looking for him. There was grief in it. Even His sometimes severe messages of judgment are but further offers of mercy. In one of the first Billy Graham evangelistic films, *Mr Texas,* there was a touching song sung by a young woman about her brother, who was putting up a stout resistance to every overture of the Saviour – "O beloved enemy"! Man is certainly an enemy, but he is a beloved enemy; none of us can tell how beloved.

This unchanging love of God for a sinful world was seen in the message of the angels on that first Christmas Day, who understood, as man did not, the true significance of the event they were celebrating. As they looked on that babe and "veiled in flesh the Godhead saw", they sang, "Glory to God in the Highest and on earth, peace, goodwill toward men."[7] They saw in God sending His Son

---

[6]Genesis 3:9.   [7]Luke 2:14.

an indication of God's goodwill to man in spite of their ill-will to Him. The old Christmas hymn has got the message right, I think,

> *"Goodwill henceforth from heaven to men*
> *Begin and never cease."*

In the days when there were rules for war and men kept to the rules, it was always an understood thing that, before one country declared war on another, it withdrew its ambassador. When the ambassador was safe home they could declare war. But that time long ago God did not withdraw His Ambassador, but sent Him, as on a blessed goodwill mission, with all the risk to Him that it would involve. What was that but a clear statement that though man was at war with God, God was at peace with man? Angels saw it on the one hand as an indication of God's glory in the highest, and on the other as His unchanged goodwill toward men on earth. Were it otherwise, He would never have sent the Lord Jesus. Men still do not believe it. Though they sing the familiar carols at Christmas, and feel a sentimental pleasure in doing so, they still resist Him and are at enmity with Him, because deep down they think He must be against them. While they think that, wild horses will not drive them to Him.

God's difficulties

If men are to be reconciled, God must address Himself to the difficult task of dispelling the sinner's guilty suspicions of Him and persuade the sinner that, though God is the moral Arbiter of the universe, He is not against him but loves him just as he is. It is not enough for Him to say, "Be ye reconciled to Me." Something must actually be done that will demonstrate that God is not as the sinner thinks He is and that will provide every encouragement for him to return to Him. Here God must take the initiative, for, if left to himself, man will never take even the first step back.

There is, however, not only this difficulty of man being willing to come back, but justice demands, "the soul that sinneth it shall die."[8] Can God disregard the claims of His own justice? If after Adam had left the Garden of Eden he had wanted to come back, what would he have found? Cherubim were standing at the East of the Garden and a flaming sword which turned every way guarded the Tree of Life.[9] Divine justice had put that sword there. Can God tell justice to sheath its sword, just because man wants to come back?

So if man is to be willing and able to respond, that which needs to be done is not only something that will dispel his guilty suspicions of God, but at the same time will satisfy that sword of justice and show God to be just in having him back.

God has done it

The good news is that God has done just that. He

---

[8]Ezekiel 18:4.   [9]Genesis 3:24.

has "devised means that His banished be not expelled from Him."[1] What is it that has been done? It is a Man nailed to a tree, dying a criminal's death. Only criminals were put to death on crosses. Who is He up there? It is God in human flesh! What is He doing undergoing death in such a fashion? Let the Apostle Paul answer; "God was in Christ reconciling the world unto Himself, not imputing their trespasses unto them."[2] Can you believe it? God is not blaming the sinner, nor imputing to him his trespasses, for the simple reason He is imputing them to Himself in the Person of His Son! Because man will not take the blame, God in His Son has done so. That is brokenness indeed on the part of the Deity. This is why the gospel declares He is not against the sinner, but for him – an attitude that men find so hard to believe, and they always will, until they see the cross and understand they are fighting One who is not fighting them.

In a quarrel between two parties there can be no reconciliation between them until the initial wrong which one perpetrated against the other is acknowledged and amends made for it. It is no good saying, "Now you two, shake hands and be friends," if that initial thing is not put right; the old feeling of enmity is still there and may well break out again in hot words.

The making of amends is the responsibility of the offending party, not the injured one. The latter might well say, "I can't put it right because I did not do it

---

[1] 2 Samuel 14:14.   [2] 2 Corinthians 5:19.

in the first place." But in this great estrangement between man and God something has been done for which there is no human precedent. It is not man the offending party who makes the amends, but God, the injured one. He does so by humbling Himself to appear in human history in the Person of His Son, charging Himself with the sins man has commited, dragging a cross up Golgotha's hill, there to die between two thieves, as if He were one Himself, thus paying the dread price of sin.

In an act of infinite grace, the offended One takes the place of the offending one. As He does so, the flaming sword of divine justice is sheathed in His breast and its fire slaked in His blood.

> *All for my sake, my peace to make*
> *Now sleeps that sword for me.*

It is not, then, a third party, Jesus, coming between man and God, but the injured party Himself who is on that cross. What a God is this! Here the true character of Deity is revealed as nowhere else.

For this reason He insists on placarding the sight of Himself on the cross before the eyes of a guilty, suspicious world, and He insists that His ambassadors in all their preaching preach the cross. As men and women see the cross, God whispers in their ears, "Now say I am against you; that I hold your sins against you, that I am your enemy, out to rob you of your happiness! Which of all your friends to save you could or would have shed his blood?" As men look, they see at last the God with whom they have to do, not One who is against them, but who is for them. For some, not all alas, their suspicions vanish, their opposition wilts and they fall at the feet of the Crucified and say, "Love so amazing, so divine, shall have my soul, my life, my all."

A beseeching God

If it is a touching sight to see God, the injured party, making amends to reconcile man, the offending party, then the sight of the same God beseeching man to receive that reconciliation and be at peace with Him, is equally touching, almost more so. It is not man beseeching God to be merciful; rather God beseeching man to be reconciled. It is not the junior pleading with the Senior; it is the Senior pleading with the junior.

That is the picture we have in the great reconciliation passage set out on the opening page of this chapter; "Now then we are ambassadors for Christ, as though God did beseech you by us: we pray you in Christ's stead, be ye reconciled to God."[3]

True, He does it through what are called His ambassadors, but it is God who is doing the beseeching through them – "as though God did beseech you by us." What an extraordinary picture it is – a beseeching God! As if He had not done enough in effecting the reconciliation, must He now beg and persuade man to receive it? It is sheer grace. Everything is the wrong way round when grace is

[3] 2 Corinthians 5:20.

on the field; not man pleading with God, but God pleading with man.

His ambassadors, through whom He does this work, were once enemies themselves, but they have been reconciled to God by the death of His Son, and have been given this ministry of reconciliation.

An ambassador represents his country to another government. As long as he is there, you know that the country that sent him is at peace with that other country. If anything goes wrong in the relationship, he is the man on the spot to deal with it and to try to effect a speedy reconciliation.

What a noble title for the one who was once himself an enemy of God! He is now an ambassador for Christ in an alien world. Although things have gone wrong between man and God – man is now at war with God – God has not withdrawn His ambassadors as would normally be the case, but has kept them to beseech men, in season and out of season, to be reconciled to God.

And the message which the ambassador brings? At first sight it would seem that it is, "We pray you in Christ's stead, be ye reconciled to God." But I suggest his message does not end there; he continues with the word, "for He hath made Him who knew no sin to be sin for us."[4] Note that little word *for*. It links the sentence that follows it with the one before it. The ambassador is giving the greatest encouragement he can for men to be reconciled to God, "*for* (or, because) this God has made Him who

---

[4] 2 Corinthians 5:21.

knew no sin to be sin for them that they might be made the righteousness of God in Him." That does not look like the work of One who is against them, but rather of One who loves them. I imagine He points almost with a sob to Calvary as the greatest encouragement for sinners to return. See the contrasted phrases, "Christ made sin" and they "made the righteousness of God in Him" – they counted right, Christ for their sakes counted wrong. A blessed judicial exchange!

Preacher, if you want scriptural ground for making your appeal to sinners, here it is. If God beseeches men, so may you.

Our response

What is the response that sinners like ourselves are called to make? It will vary according to which of the Great Words of the Gospel we are looking at. In some cases it will be the response of faith; in other cases it will be the response of repentance; in yet others it will be to give up self-effort and to appropriate Christ. But here I think the response will be to give up running away and going on my own path and to allow Christ to take over. In other words, to lay down the arms of my rebellion and bring the enmity and unwillingness to an end. This was certainly the response I made when I first became a Christian. There was not much intelligent faith or repentance about it. I had been having a running battle with God for a year, and at last I gave up my resistance to Him.

The French admiral who was defeated at the

Battle of the Nile came on board Nelson's flagship to make his surrender. Dressed in his finery and with a smile on his face, he extended his hand to Nelson, but Nelson did not extend his. "Your sword first," said Nelson. The French admiral withdrew his sword from its scabbard and handed it hilt first to Nelson, who took it and snapped it across his knee; only then did he shake hands with the Frenchman. "Your sword first," is ever the Lord's demand as a man takes his first step to reconciliation with God.

Then comes faith in the blood of Jesus, that is, he dares to believe that because of what Jesus did for him on the cross, he is dead to the power of his sins to condemn him any longer and he is free and alive to God. The door of the heart is swung open to Jesus and everything is turned over to Him.

Twofold reconciliation

It is only part of the work of the cross to reconcile man to God; the other part is to reconcile man to his fellowman. The great passage on this twofold reconciliation is in Ephesians chapter two. Three times we have the phrase "both ... one".[5]

When a person is reconciled to God, he is well on the way to being reconciled to the other man who has been bothering him; he will look at everyone with new eyes. If, at the same time, another with whom he is in contact, (or with whom he lives) is reconciled to God, they are going to meet at the cross

---

[5]Ephesians 2:14.

and there is going to be a beautiful experience of this twofold reconciliation – with God and with one another.

The annals of the gospel are full of such glorious stories and I have to restrain myself from filling up pages with them. Suffice it to say that this is the way in which marriages are saved, families with teenagers reunited, church splits healed and harmony restored in office and factory. These are what Charles Wesley called, "the triumphs of His grace."

It is important that we should know this twofold reconciliation, because our relationship with God and our fellows go together, and the former is no better than the latter. If I am wrong with my fellow, to that extent I am wrong with God. Could it be a matter of relationships which is holding you up in your Christian life? For your encouragement, this is an area where Jesus excels. It is His ability to make "both … one" that constitutes His fame as a Saviour.

Middle wall of partion

In Ephesians chapter two Paul applies the matter of the twofold reconciliation to the big divide that existed between Jews and Gentiles. The division was caused by what Paul called "the law of commandments contained in ordinances",[6] the Mosaic laws and rituals, which applied to the Jews, but not to the Gentiles. It was "the middle wall of

---

[6]Ephesians 2:15.

partition", the Jews being on one side and the Gentiles on the other; it bred enmity between them, the Jews despising the Gentiles and the Gentiles resenting the Jews.

Paul's argument is that Jesus has broken down the middle wall of partition by abolishing in His flesh the law of commandments contained in ordinances, which was the basic cause of the enmity. He abolished it in His flesh, that is by His atoning death, which by its very nature made nothing of status, distinction, privilege and religious observance, as being of any value in the restoring of a man's relationship with God. Jesus achieved man's reconciliation by His work on the cross. A man's advantages, religious or secular, are no advantage, and his disadvantages, religious or secular, are no disadvantage either; grace makes the gift available without any reference to either the one or the other. Before the wondrous cross a man learns to "pour contempt on all his pride." Three blessed results follow.

First, "for to make in Himself of the two one new man".[7] There is no distinction now between ordained and laity, or any other discriminating mark, religious, social or racial. All have been reconciled to God in one body by the cross, and therefore to one another.

Second, "having slain the enmity thereby". Where the cross is embraced as the ground of reconciliation, the enmity between warring groups is slain.

Thirdly, "so making peace" – not only reconciled

---

[7]Ephesians 2:15.

with God, but with one another, and loving one another.

First be reconciled to thy brother

From what the Lord teaches in the Sermon on the Mount we are to make the matter of being reconciled to our brother a priority. "Therefore if thou bring thy gift to the altar, and there rememberest that thy brother hath aught against thee; leave there thy gift before the altar and go thy way; *first* be reconciled to thy brother, and then come and offer thy gift."[8] Please note that the situation the Lord has in mind is one where we remember that our brother has something against us. We may not have anything against him, but he has something against us and we know it. We are not at peace about something we have said or done with regard to him, and it bothers us as we seek to offer God the gift of our service. So important is it to get right with him (it could affect our whole Christian walk if we don't) that we are to give it priority; *first* be reconciled to your brother and then offer your gift.

How shall we be reconciled to him? The next verse tells us; "Agree with thine adversary quickly."[9] It does not need a long discussion, much of which would probably be spent justifying and explaining ourselves, but simply "agree with thine adversary quickly" and say with regard to that which you said or did, "Brother, sister, you were

---

[8]Matthew 5:23, 24.   [9]Matthew 5:25.

right in objecting to me, and I was wrong; I ask for your forgiveness." Let us not plead any extenuating circumstances, but be content to be the only sinner in the matter. It is not enough to say you are sorry; you need to ask for forgiveness, and then stop talking. The ball then is in the other's court; what you need now for it to be finished is the other person's forgiveness. It is sometimes as hard for someone to grant forgiveness as it is for you to ask for it. A broken and contrite spirit is needed. But Jesus went lower than this for us, and we will have Him with us in it. He will without doubt help the other person and another relationship will be healed and we will be in the enjoyment of this twofold reconciliation again.

"We pray you in Christ's stead, be ye reconciled to God."

"For by grace are ye saved through faith; and that not of yourselves: it is the gift of God: not of works, lest any man should boast" (Ephesians 2:8, 9).

"And if by grace, then it is no more of works: otherwise grace is no more grace" (Romans 11:6).

4

GRACE
for the undeserving

There is no good news for us sinners if God is not seen as a God of grace. This great word is so foundational and pervasive in my own personal thinking, that it has already seeped into the first three chapters of this book, and anticipated somewhat this chapter specially devoted to it.

What is grace? It is an element in the divine character, the chiefest and most beautiful of all God's attributes. It is the undeserved love of God, with special emphasis on its being undeserved. For that reason it is always put in contrast to works. "If by grace, then it is no more of works: otherwise grace is no more grace."[1]

The moment we have to improve ourselves and become more morally suitable to be saved, or, if already saved, more deeply blessed, then grace is no more grace. As it says in Romans, "To him that worketh is the reward not reckoned of grace, but of debt."[2] Indeed, to try to be a better and more active Christian in order to experience renewal is nothing

---

[1] Romans 11:6.   [2] Romans 4:4.

more than an attempt to put God in our debt, so that He owes us His blessing. This is impossible and something God will never have. Paul says in another passage, quoting from Job, "Who hath first given to Him and it shall be recompensed to him again?"[3] The answer to that question is, no one. We must come as beggars to a God of grace and content ourselves to live on charity. No one likes to live on charity, but with God you will never be saved in any other way, nor after salvation will you be able to enjoy the further blessings of the Christian life on any other ground.

It is not only positive demerit in the recipient that makes grace, grace, but also the greatness of what is given, so undeserved, so uncalled for and sometimes so unexpected, and above all, out of all proportion to what a man has tried to do.

Freely by His Grace

Another verse that further defines grace is, "being justified freely by His grace."[4] The Greek word "freely" is elsewhere translated, "without a cause", as where Jesus says, "they hated Me without a cause."[5] Therefore the text could be read, "being justified without a cause by His grace." His love for me and justification of me as a sinner were as much without a cause as was our hatred of Him. I no more deserved His love than He deserved our hatred. There was nothing of good in me to cause Him to

---

[3]Romans 11:35.   [4]Romans 3:24.   [5]John 15:25.

take me as a sinner and justify me. His deeds and ours were completely gratuitous. That word, gratuitous, is another translation of the same Greek word. God justified me gratuitously, expecting nothing in return. That is grace. As the hymn says,

> Jesus what didst Thou find in me
> That Thou hast dealt so lovingly?

He didn't find a thing. There was not found in me any procuring cause for Him to save me. Perhaps the best translation for ordinary reading is in the R.S.V., "being justified by His grace as a gift". Not only is our initial justification "by His grace as a gift", but every other experience of blessing is going to be by the same way, "by His grace as a gift."

Grace and love

There is a difference between love and grace. All grace is love, but not all love is necessarily grace. It is conceivable for love to be bestowed on someone because there is much about him or her which is good, attractive and meritorious. In a case like that such love could never be said to be grace. The love of God only becomes the grace of God when it has for its object one who patently does not deserve it. Then love acquires this glorious new name, grace.

The difference between the grace of God and the love of God is to my mind illustrated by the difference between the sunshine and the rainbow. What a beautiful thing is the sunshine, coming out of a cloudless blue sky and bathing everything with its brilliance! This is a fit emblem of the love of God, of His benificence to all His creation, willing everyone and everything nothing but good. The hymn, "Summer suns are glowing over land and sea", certainly views the sunshine as a picture of the love of God. But when the sunlight shines through rain on to dark clouds beyond, it is split into its component hues and we have one of the most beautiful phenonema of nature, the rainbow. It is still sunlight, but the difference has come about by that on which it shines, rain and clouds, and the resultant rainbow is even more beautiful than the sunlight that produced it. So when the love of God has for its object the guilty and the undeserving, shedding their tears and breathing their sighs, it becomes the grace of God as He undertakes to supply their need. Revelation chapter four tells us that "there was a rainbow round about the throne."[6] There always is!

This is our God, the God of all grace and that grace is the brightest jewel in His crown of glory. The angels marvel over it and the redeemed love Him for it. Grace makes Him not only reachable, but lovable. "I love the Lord," said David, "because He hath heard my cry."[7] Though he knew he did not deserve to be heard.

---

[6]Revelation 4:1   [7]Psalm 116:1.

Grace and law

We cannot speak of grace without speaking of law, for in the epistles grace is always put in contrast to law. The contrast is definitely stated in some places (as "Ye are not under the law, but under grace"[8]) and implied in others.

Here we are not speaking of grace merely as an element in the divine character, but as the principle on which God reckons the believer righteous in His sight. There are two possible principles on which this could be done, the ground of grace, or the ground of law; the old covenant of the law and the new covenant of grace.[9]

The old covenant points us back to Mount Sinai where God through Moses gave His moral law, being the "Thou shalt … thou shalt not" of the ten commandments and much else. The covenant based on law was simply, "This do and thou shalt live."[1] But it was implied, "This fail to do and thou shalt die" – ominous thought!

This covenant, shorn of its Judiastic rituals, is still the covenant that the natural man understands best. The man in the street, if he thinks about his relationship with God at all, thinks of it on the basis of an exterior code of ethics which he must obey. "This do and thou shalt live" is simple and clear to him. Do the best you can, do not harm anybody, fulfil your duty, and if there is a God, He will be pleased with

---

[8]Romans 6:14.   [9]Galatians 4:22–26 and Hebrews 8:7–13.
[1]Exodus 19:5, 6 and Romans 10:5.

you; and if there is a heaven, you will go there.

This is also the covenant to which the Christian gravitates after his conversion all too readily. "This do, and thou shalt live" is the system so often under which he now seeks to run his Christian life. It is so natural to feel that, to be more deeply blessed, to find fuller peace with God, to be more greatly used by Him in His service, we must approximate more nearly to the highest standards of a holy life, spend more time in prayer, be more involved in Christian service and so on. How else can we expect blessing from God, if not on this principle? Of course, our thinking is not always so clearly expressed as this, but all sorts of attitudes we adopt and things we do are really subtle variants. At first it all sounds fine and it seems the promised blessing is only just round the corner.

But what if we fail? What if we never succeed in attaining? Then, obviously, the other side of the covenant must come into force: "This fail to do, and thou shalt die."[2] The fact is, we have not done them, we have not attained, not even the most consecrated of us, and all we have inherited from that old covenant is death – that is, reproach and condemnation. We feel we must make another attempt to try harder; but we only fail again, to be involved in an even deeper sense of guilt. Ultimately we come to the place where we begin to doubt if we were ever saved at all, and we lose the assurance of our salvation.

Actually, this law-instilled guilt is precisely what

---

[2]Deuteronomy 30:15–17.

was intended, for in this way "the law becomes our schoolmaster to bring us unto Christ that we might be justified by faith".

Under the law with its ten-fold lash,
*   Learning, alas, how true,*
That the more I tried, the sooner I died,
*   While the law cried, You! You! You!*

Hopelessly still did the battle rage,
*   O, wretched man, my cry!*
And deliverance I sought, by some penance bought,
*   While my heart cried, I! I! I!*

Then came a day when my struggling ceased
*   And, trembling in every limb,*
At the foot of the tree, where One died for me,
*   My heart cried, Him! Him! Him!*

How different is the covenant of grace which, interestingly, antedated that of law by four hundred years. Being of grace, its blessings are offered gratuitously with nothing expected in return. Here men do not work to get righteousness (vain hope!), but rather they already have it imputed to them as a gift because they have been made right with God by the blood of Jesus.

Best of all, when a man sees grace he gains a complete assurance of his salvation which he never had while he was living under law, dependent on whether he had attained or not. This is clearly taught in the verse, "Therefore it is of faith that it might be by grace, to the end the promise might be sure to all the seed".[3] Lack of assurance is not always due to a person looking for feelings instead of taking God at His word. More often it is because he is living under law, not knowing whether or not he has come up to the standard. This verse gives us the real ground for assurance; it is of faith that it might be by grace, where no works are required and where the recipient can be sure by faith.

Grace and truth

We must include the important statement by the Apostle John in his gospel, "The law was given by Moses, but grace and truth came by Jesus Christ".[4]

Most readers of the New Testament are familiar with the fact that the teaching about law and grace is very much the province of the Apostle Paul. It is everywhere in his two great epistles, to the Romans and to the Galatians, and in other places, too. But I have found that John, too, speaks of law and grace and the truths are as foundational to John as to Paul.

John puts grace as much in contrast to law as Paul does, but he links truth with grace. He says that not only has grace come by Jesus Christ, but truth too, and sets them both in contrast to the law, which had come by Moses. This mixture of grace and truth makes everything come alive.

The word, truth, can be used in two ways. It is often used to denote doctrine, the message of the

---

[3]Romans 4:16.   [4]John 1:17.

gospel. But in other places, especially in John's writings, it means reality, correspondence with things as they are, honestly. Indeed, used in this sense, it is one of John's favourite words. Here he tells us that it is not only grace that has come by Jesus Christ, but truth, too, and that, by implication, through the cross. If the cross of Jesus is the supreme revelation of grace, so it is of truth – the truth about God and especially the truth about ourselves.

The truth about us all stares down at us from the cross. It was on a cross that He died and if death on a cross was a punishment reserved for criminals, which it was under Roman law, and if it was our place that He took, what does that make us to be? Nothing more than a lot of criminals! That is the truth about all of us and it is revealed by the place the Lord had to take to save us. What grace, you say: yes, but what humbling truth for us too!

It is only as we admit to the truth of being criminals in God's sight that we qualify for His grace. How skilfully the Apostle John balances his message. If it is only grace that has come by Jesus Christ, then the message might seem too sugary and soft. If it is grace and truth that has come, then we are not going to be let off anything; all is going to be revealed. But with that revelation, there is plenteous grace to cover all our sins.

> *Thus while His death my sin displays,*
>   *In all its blackest hue,*
> *Such is the mystery of grace*
>   *It seals my pardon too.*

All God's approaches to us are with this mixture of grace and truth, but He will vary the mixture according to our need at the time. On one occasion we may feel down and discouraged because of our shortcomings and more than usually prone to take a stick to ourselves. Then God will see to it that the message will come to us with a bigger mixture of grace – "Be of good cheer, thy sins be forgiven thee."[5] On another occasion we may be tolerating sin, presuming on grace, perhaps compromising. In that case the message that will come to us will be rather more heavy on the truth as God sees it to be. Our hearts will be searched and sin be revealed – only that we might repent again and thus qualify all the more for proffered mercy. But all the time grace is the main emphasis. "Let your speech be always with grace, seasoned with salt."[6] Grace is the main ingredient, truth the necessary seasoning, varied according to present need, both in our relationship with one another and in God's relationship with us.

As we have said, the word "truth" is a characteristic word with the Apostle John. It keeps on occurring in his writings, in each different place with something special to say. In his Gospel he says, "For everyone that doeth evil, hateth the light, neither cometh to the light lest his deeds should be reproved, but he that doeth truth cometh to the light that his deeds may be made manifest that they are wrought in God."[7] Now it is understandable that the man who has done wrong will shun the light

---

[5]Matthew 9:2.   [6]Colossians 4:6.   [7]John 3:20, 21.

and will want to hide what he has done. But the interest of this passage is in the contrast, "but he that doeth truth." That is a strange contrast, isn't it? You would have thought that the contrast would be between "he that doeth evil" and "he that doeth good". But it does not say that, but rather "he that doeth truth".

The meaning is that before we ever try to do good to make up for what we have done wrong, we are to "do truth", that is, be plain honest with ourselves, and where necessary with others and, of course, with God, about the wrong we have done. Before we ever try to do anything to compensate for the wrong that we have done, we must admit the wrong we have done, that is "do truth", that is be plain honest about it. The opposite then of doing evil is doing truth. That is what God wants of us. Then we shall be unafraid of coming into the light and it will be made manifest "that our deeds are wrought in God". What are the deeds that are wrought in God? This "doing truth" , this honesty about sin. Having "done truth", we may know that grace has come too and pardoned the wrong. Then we can go forward to do good and put things right in the strength that God supplies. So be sure before you do good that you "do truth"!

Grace and repentance

Sometimes the thoughtful listener is disturbed when he hears grace preached as fully as this. He is disturbed lest this might lead to what is sometimes called "cheap grace". But grace can look after itself. Grace does not let the sinner down, but on the other hand it does not let the sinner off. There is another side to the coin of grace. Although the adjective linked today with grace is often the word "amazing" (as in the well-known hymn, "Amazing grace how sweet the sound"), to qualify for grace you must admit you are wrong and take the sinner's place. There is nothing so humbling as that. Sometimes a man dies a veritable death when he confesses himself wrong where before he said he was right. Nothing cheap about that! Grace makes this demand because of its very character, that it is good news for bad people. You have to confess you are bad to be a candidate. Only self-confessed wrong ones are true candidates. That is why the way of works is so popular because people are wanting a way to get right without having to humble themselves. But "he that humbleth himself shall be exalted"[8] – every time! That is how it always works out under grace.

Further, grace gives us every inducement to repent in the way the law does not. In view of the terms of the covenant from Mount Sinai, you cannot afford to be wrong there; if you are wrong at Sinai, you are in for a thrashing! Therefore we always justify ourselves. But at Calvary things are different: "Mercy there is great and grace is free; pardon there is multiplied to me." We can afford to admit we are wrong because then we are forgiven and declared right with God.

---

[8]Luke 14:11.

Solid peace is restored to us. A preacher friend once said this deep truth: "Where there is no revival, everybody is right; but when revival comes, that is, when Jesus comes, everyone is wrong." Then the self-confessed wrong ones are declared right with God through the blood of His Son and they know it! Be assured then, repentance and revival only come with the rediscovery of grace.

Grace and holiness

I can imagine that my thoughtful reader may still not be satisfied and be saying, "Might not all this lead to irresponsibility amongst Christians where they do the very thing Paul counselled them against when he said, 'We beseech you that ye receive not the grace of God in vain'?"[9] Yes, it might. Men can abuse grace, but that is the calculated risk God takes. If He tightened up on grace and introduced all sorts of extra conditions to be fulfilled, whereas it might prove salutary for some, it would make others despair, perhaps the greater number, for they might feel it was beyond their feeble resources. So God has decided to let grace be grace, and to attach no strings to it. If grace does not produce holiness, He has no other way.

But it does produce holiness. He to whom grace forgives much, loves much. He who loves much cannot do enough for the One who has forgiven him so much – but not, mark you, as a legal

---

[9] 2 Corinthians 6:1.

requirement. This is what Paul meant when he said, "Faith worketh by love".[1] He had been asserting that the justification of the sinner before God is not by works, but by faith. He knew that some would say, "That is letting people off; none will bother to do good works." Paul, in effect answers by saying, "Fear not, those justified by faith will work all right. Faith in grace generates love, and love knows no limit as to what it will do for the Loved One."

So if we are working little for the Lord, it is because we love little; and if we love little, it is because we have been forgiven little; and if we have been forgiven little, it is because we have been repenting little. So we had better start on that right now. It is true Paul said to the Corinthian Christians, "We beseech you that ye receive not the grace of God in vain." But he knew that as soon as the much-forgiven realised what they had been doing (receiving the grace of God in vain), they would repent and get right quickly.

The simple fact is that grace produces results, love to God, holiness and service, results that the law, that is, a mere sense of legal obligation, never does. As you observe the results of the message of grace in people's lives you will find yourself saying, "Praise God, it works!"

The prophet Elisha refused to take a gift from Naaman the leper in return for his healing – that was certainly grace. The result? Naaman said, "Thy

---

[1]Galatians 5:6.

servant will henceforth offer neither burnt offering nor sacrifice unto other gods, but unto Jehovah." Coming from a Gentile general, up till then ignorant of Israel's God, that was surely one of the great conversions of the Old Testament. Elisha did not get his present, but he got his man. Another victory of grace!

Grace instead of grace

The Apostle John wrote, "Of His fulness have all we received and grace instead of grace" (literal Greek);[2] not as you might have expected, grace instead of sin, but grace instead of grace. It gives us the picture of ourselves standing on a river bank, looking down on the flowing waters. It is a beautiful sight; we can even see the fish and we would gladly retain that view. However, it soon flows past and that particular water is gone – but only to be replaced by another quantity of water carrying its own special beauty. It is water instead of water.

So is the grace of God. From the point of view of the recipient it is not just an isolated experience, which at all costs he must retain and which, if it seems to disappear, he must do his best to recover. It is rather like a continuously flowing river, which means he can afford to let the first experience go, for there is plenty more where that came from. There is grace instead of grace.

---

[2]John 1:16.

When we have exhausted our store of endurance,
When our strength has failed 'ere the day is half gone,
When we reach the end of our hoarded resources,
Our Father's full giving is only begun.

His love has no limit, His grace has no measure,
His power no boundary known unto men,
For out off His infinite riches in Jesus,
He giveth and giveth and giveth again.

Annie Johnson Flint

"The life of the flesh is in the blood: and I have given it to you upon the altar to make an atonement for your souls: for it is the blood that maketh an atonement for the soul" (Leviticus 17:11).

"In that day there shall be a fountain opened to the house of David and to the inhabitants of Jerusalem for sin and for uncleanness" (Zechariah 13:1).

"He entered in once for all into the holy place, having obtained eternal redemption for us. For if the blood of bulls and of goats, and the ashes of an heifer sprinkling the unclean, sanctifieth to the purifying of the flesh: how much more shall the blood of Christ, who through the eternal Spirit offered Himself without spot to God, cleanse your conscience from dead works to serve the living God?" (Hebrews 9:12–14).

"Having therefore, brethren, boldness to enter into the Holiest by the blood of Jesus … Let us draw near with a true heart in full assurance of faith" (Hebrews 10:19, 22).

"But if we walk in the light, as He is in the light, we have fellowship one with another, and the blood of Jesus Christ, His Son, cleanseth us from all sin." (1 John 1:7).

5

BLOOD
for the remission of sin

When we read the Bible it does not take us long to discover there is a red line running through it from beginning to end. There is constant reference to blood and to redemption by blood in both Old and New Testaments. Don't dismiss that word, but give it your special attention. It is one of the great words of the gospel. Indeed it is the foundation of all the other great words we shall consider and alone makes it possible for God to extend His good news to bad people, for "it is the blood that maketh an atonement for the soul" and without such blood-shedding there is no remission.

I understand that Alpine mountaineers, who need to be roped together in their climbing, have to use a rope of very high specification and that such ropes are distinguished by a thin red line running through them, as a sign they are up to standard. That is an illustration of the red line of redemption by the blood of Jesus which runs through the Bible from Genesis to Revelation, in prophecy, typology, or fulfilment; from the blood sacrifice which Abel offered, and which God accepted rather than Cain's, right through the blood offerings of the Law of Moses and on through the prophecies of the Messiah in the Psalms and the Prophets, and through the Gospels with their story of the cross, and on through the theology of the Epistles, to the great cry of praise to the Lamb in the Book of Revelation: "Thou art worthy … for Thou wast slain and hast redeemed us to God by Thy blood out of every kindred and tongue and people and nation."[1]

It is not only we readers of a later date who can discern from our perspective the red line, but the writer of the letter to the Hebrews did, too. He wrote, "And almost all things are under the law cleansed by blood, and without shedding of blood is no remission."[2]

How powerful that last word is, made all the more so by being put negatively! Had it been put positively, "by shedding of blood there is remission", it would not have been so powerful and final as, "without shedding of blood is no remission." That shuts every avenue to God but the way of the blood, reminding us of the cherubim that God put at the East of the garden of Eden "with a flaming sword which turned every way to keep the way of the Tree of Life." The message of the cherubim that day was, no way back! But the next time they appear in Scripture, they proclaim a very different message. Two golden images of them stand in the tabernacle of the wilderness, overshadowing the Mercy Seat with their faces one toward another, but looking

[1]Revelation 5:9. [2]Hebrews 9:22.

down on the blood-stained Mercy Seat. In the blood, sprinkled once a year on the Mercy Seat, their swords have been sheathed, prophetically, in the breast and in the blood of God's own Son, giving remission for all. The message of the cherubim is plain, both negatively and positively; you can come no other way, but even you can come this way, the way of the blood; and they stand to welcome all who do so.

> *Jehovah bade His sword awake,*
> *O Christ, it woke 'gainst Thee!*
> *Thy blood the flaming blade must slake;*
> *Thy heart its sheath must be –*
> *All for my sake, my peace to make;*
> *Now sleeps that sword for me.*

Not only is the theme of the blood dominant in Scripture, but it is also dominant in the church's hymnology. Often the fullest exposition of its meaning is to be found in some of the great hymns of the church and the later hymns of revival – though it is a sad fact that today each new hymn book seems to contain even fewer hymns about the blood. But in times of revival the doctrine of the blood of Christ always comes into new prominence in experience, in teaching and in testimony.

This is so within the only revival which I personally have had deep touch with, that in East Africa, which has continued in an ever-growing way from 1930 right up to the time of writing. The constant song of the brethren there is, "Oh, the cleansing blood has reached me, glory, glory to the Lamb." If I heard it once on my various visits, I heard it time and again, and it is sung nearly always in celebration of a new triumph of the Lamb in somebody's life as he shares his testimony.

What does it really mean?

It is well that we pause and enquire as to the real meaning of the phrase, "the blood of Jesus" and how it is that the message of the blood is so central in doctrine and experience. We should be aware that to many people, even to believers, constant use of the term is offensive and they would much prefer to speak about the death of Christ, or the cross of Christ, and it could become a meaningless cliché if we never explained the special significance that Scripture attaches to the expression. The death of Christ, and the cross of Christ and the blood of Christ are not interchangeable terms, and if God in a certain context speaks about the blood of His Son, it is because that phrase expresses there a certain aspect of truth.

There are two Old Testament types which will help us at this point. By using the word, "type", I mean what the Oxford dictionary means by it: "a person, thing, or event. which serves as an illustration, symbol, or prophetic similitude of another thing."

Passover

The first is the Passover and the blood-sprinkled doorposts in Egypt. The background of the incident was God's declaration, "I will pass through the land of Egypt this night and will smite all the firstborn in the land of Egypt, both man and beast; and against all the gods of Egypt I will execute judgment." In preparation for this great event each Hebrew home was bidden to take a lamb, slay it and with hyssop (a common herb) as a brush, sprinkle its blood on the doorposts and the upper lintels of the houses where they were, with the assurance from God, "When I see the blood I will pass over you and not suffer the destroyer to come into your houses to smite your firstborn."[3] In the middle of God's instructions about the matter there comes an all-important phrase, which explains the efficacy of the blood more than any other I know, "And the blood shall be to you for a token upon the houses where ye are."[4]

Apparently, it was not the physical blood that was so important, but that of which it was a token, of judgment met. The decree had gone out that divine justice was to fall on every house in Egypt, except in the case of the Hebrews. Their being spared was not on the ground of being Hebrews, but on the gound of the blood they had sprinkled. Apart from that blood, judgment would have entered their homes as certainly as those of the Egyptians. But that blood

[3]Exodus 12:23. [4]Exodus 12:13.

was a token of the fact that judgment had already been executed as far as they were concerned.

I like to think that as the sun was setting, fathers and sons went out of the doors, each father with a lamb, taken from the sheep or from the goats, and that as a father was about to kill it his son remonstrated. It had been in the house four days, according to instructions, and perhaps had become something of a household pet. But the father, I imagine, says, "Son, either this lamb dies, or you will." So he killed it, and sprinkled the blood of the lamb on the doorposts and the lintel. It was there as a token, a token that judgment as far as that home was concerned had already been there; it had fallen on the lamb instead of on the son. So that night passed peacefully for the son, for God saw the blood and was faithful to His word; He stood protector over the home and did not suffer the destroying angel to enter; and all because He saw the blood upon the door.

This passage is one of the great Old Testament types of Christ. The well-known verses in Peter's epistle where he speaks of us being redeemed from our vain manner of life by "the precious blood of Christ, as of a lamb without blemish and without spot, who verily was foreordained before the foundation of the world, but was manifest in these last times for you"[5] clearly authenticates it as such.

Being the clear type it is, the words "and the blood shall be to you for a token" throw a flood of light on

---

[5]1 Peter 1:18–20.

the matter we are considering. As in the type so in the antitype; it is not the physical, or historical blood of Christ, that is important but that of which it was and is a token; it is for us a token of judgment met. The judgment that was our due has fallen on Jesus on the cross and been exhausted by Him there, and that to the entire satisfaction of God. There is a verse in the epistle to the Hebrews where it imagines the blood of Jesus speaking: "the blood of Jesus speaketh better things than that of Abel."[6] And what does it say? It is all the time repeating, first in God the Father's ears and then to the believer, those words Jesus uttered on the cross. "It is finished"[7]; that is, sin's judgment has been met. No more of human merit is needed for complete remission. It is "one sacrifice for sins for ever"; the blood is an everlasting token of the finished work of Christ.

"The best robe of heaven He bids thee put on.
Oh, could'st thou be better arrayed!"

Ashes of a heifer

The second type of the blood of Jesus in the Old Testament to which I would draw your special attention is the ritual of the ashes of the heifer, set out in Numbers chapter 19 and clearly applied to the blood of Jesus in the epistle to the Hebrews. This is not as familiar to most of us as the type of the Passover lamb just considered, but none the less

---

[6]Hebrews 12:24.   [7]John 19:30.

important. In this Numbers passage Moses is concerned with the cleansing of one who has been ceremonially defiled (contact with any form of death brought defilement under the law) and provision was made for his cleansing and reinstatment. A red heifer had been slain, its blood sprinkled on the altar and its carcass burned and reduced to ashes and carefully preserved, perhaps several barrels full, as the precious cleansing medium for the children of Israel. Whenever a defiled man wanted to be cleansed, he would ask a "clean" Israelite to perform a ceremony on him. His friend would take some of the ashes of the heifer, mingle them with water and with some hyssop as a brush, sprinkle them on him – and he would be clean.[8]

You might pass over this Mosaic ritual as one of the many things that do not have much meaning for us today, except that we find a strange and compelling reference to it in the Hebrews epistle in the New Testament. "And if the ashes of an heifer sprinkling the unclean sanctifieth to the purifying of the flesh, how much more shall the blood of Christ, who through the eternal Spirit offered Himself without spot to God, cleanse your conscience from dead works to serve the living God?"[9] That verse alone is enough to identify the ashes of the heifer as a prophetic type of the blood of Jesus Christ.

This whole imagery seems somewhat strange to us. I remember the day I saw and understood it. As I walked up and down in my study I said, "I see it, I

---

[8]Numbers 19:9–12.   [9]Hebrews 9:13, 14.

see it. You can't burn ashes. Ashes are what is left when the fire has done its work. It is a memorial to a fire that has gone out." Even so is the blood of Jesus a memorial, a token, of a fire that has gone out. The fire of the wrath of God against human sin burnt itself out in the body of our Lord Jesus, and His blood is the constant token of the fact that nothing is left of that judgment for the believer but its ashes. Therefore it cleanses his conscience from dead works and all else that condemns him, and liberates him to serve the living God. It was for me a new picture of what the finished work of Christ is to which nothing of human merit has to be added. I cannot remember clearly at this distance, but I think I did a little jig in my study!

Whiter than snow

David, living as he did before the Messiah, could not have seen in this ordinance of Moses what we do who know the story of the cross. But I am amazed at what he did see. In his great penitential psalm in which he asked for and received restoration to God after his double sin of adultery and murder, he prayed, "Purge me with hyssop, and I shall be clean; wash me and I shall be whiter than snow."[1] The first part of that verse puzzled me for long: "purge me with hyssop". First of all, the word, purge: it gave me the impression of scrubbing and rubbing, a hard process, it seemed to me – until I found out it should

---

[1]Psalm 51:7.

have been translated by the simple, familiar word, "cleanse."

As I looked at the marginal references in my Bible, which show similar verses in other parts, I was referred to Numbers 19:18, to this very ritual of the ashes of the heifer sprinkling the unclean with the hyssop brush. The reference to the hyssop gave me the clue. Hyssop was used on the Passover night, but cleansing was not in view there. But hyssop was also used for the sprinkling of the ashes of the heifer where cleansing was very much in view; indeed it was the whole object of the ritual. Without any doubt David had the latter of the two hyssop incidents in mind when he prayed.

I do not think David was asking for a literal sprinkling of the ashes on him, but he wanted the spiritual counterpart of what was symbolised. My sins are so bad, I think he said to himself, that I need a cleansing that has got fire in it, but a fire that has gone out, like that old ordinance of Moses. So he prayed, "Cleanse me as with hyssop and I shall be clean."

But then he went on to pray further; and what a stunning prayer it was! "Wash me and I shall be whiter than snow." Can anything be whiter than that? Yes, there can be – it is the heart and conscience washed in the blood of Jesus Christ. Adam's condition before he fell could be described as white as snow, but the blood-washed are made whiter than snow. They are restored to a better state than that from which Adam fell. We shall think in greater detail in our chapter on cleansing what whiter than snow means, but the great truth is that you cannot be more white in God's sight than what the blood of Jesus makes you when you call sin, sin; the fire has gone out, the work has been finished.

It is, however, not only cleansing that comes to us by the blood of Jesus, but all the other blessings of the gospel: forgiveness by His blood (not the same as cleansing, as we will see in a later chapter); peace with God by His blood; justification by His blood (that is, imputed righteousness before God); boldness to enter the Holy of Holies of His presence by His blood; the overcoming of Satan by His blood. All these and much else are made available to us by the power of His blood, when we take the sinner's place. But we must never forget that the blood of Jesus only avails for sin confessed as sin.

Sufficient for God?

Jesus by His blood settled for our sins on the cross "to the entire satisfaction of God". When you think of the appalling nature of people's sins, all crying out for justice, is it possible for Jesus to have made one sacrifice for sins for ever, and for that to be enough for God? I know it says it in the Bible, but I can understand some people having difficulty with this. It is not always the enormity of a sin that makes peace difficult to come by, but also the sensitivity of the individual conscience of the sinner. Some people have terrific battles over matters which others would consider trivial, even laughable. But the conflict is not small for the person undergoing it. In

counselling others in such conditions I have sometimes had to say, "If God is satisfied with what His
Son did for you on the cross, why can't you be?" He
is satisfied and has declared Himself so in the most
convincing way possible – in that He raised Jesus
our Lord from the dead.

The epistle to the Romans tells how Abraham
dared to believe God when He promised the impossible, that he should have a son even though Sarah
was beyond the age for child-bearing. He had a
struggle to believe it, but he did ultimately "against
hope believe in hope",[2] and reckoned that it would
indeed be so. Therefore it was counted to him for a
righteousness he did not otherwise possess. "Now it
was not written for his sake alone that it was
imputed to him, but for us also to whom it shall also
be imputed if we believe on Him that raised up
Jesus our Lord from the dead; who was delivered
for our offences, and was *raised again for our justification*".[3] God raised Jesus from the dead as a declaration that every debt was fully paid and that He was
eternally satisfied with the blood of His Son on our
behalf.

> *"If Jesus had not paid the debt,*
> *He ne'er had been at freedom set."*

That is why the Apostle Paul wrote "that if thou
shalt confess with thy mouth Jesus as Lord and
believe in thine heart that God hath raised Him from

---

[2]Romans 4:18.   [3]Romans 4:23–25.

the dead, thou shalt be saved."[4] I used to think that Paul had not put that very well. I would have put it, "if thou shalt confess with thy mouth … and believe in thine heart that Jesus has died for thee." But that would have left a major matter unsettled; was the blood enough? Was God, the final Moral Arbiter of the universe, satisfied with what Jesus had done on my behalf? If that had not been clearly settled, my conscience would not be at rest. Conscience is inexorable and if there is any query to raise, it will raise it. But in that Jesus "was brought again from the dead by the blood of the everlasting covenant",[5] it was proof that there was power in the blood and that it is enough. This is why the work of Christ on the cross is called the finished work of Christ.

> *It is surely sufficient for me,*
> *It is surely sufficient for me,*
> *If the blood of Christ is sufficient for God,*
> *It is surely sufficient for me.*

This chorus was written by an American minister of music who had been sitting under this message. He handed me both the words and music as a result of what he had been learning and of the new liberty into which he had entered. Whenever I have introduced it around the world, others have been liberated too.

---

[4]Romans 10:9. [5]Hebrews 13:20.

Sprinkling of the blood

We have been thinking of the blood shed, but the blood must be sprinkled, that is, applied. The shedding of the blood of Jesus was God's work, for it happened by divine appointment, but the sprinkling of that blood on our own consciences with regard to our own sin is something that we must do. If we don't, then the shedding of Jesus' blood is in vain as far as our personal experience is concerned. The importance of the subject can be seen by the fact that the sprinkling of the blood in both Old and New Testaments is referred to no less than 41 times!

We have already seen how the blood was sprinkled on the Passover night in Egypt and the ashes of a heifer (symbolising the blood) were sprinkled on the ceremonially unclean. But under the Mosiac law blood was sprinkled on much else – on altars, on Aaron on the day of his consecration as high priest, on the book of the covenant as Moses read it to the people, and on the people as they listened to it, on lepers in the day of their reinstatement, and so on.

There are three important references in the New Testament to the sprinkling of the blood of Jesus Christ. The first is in Hebrews chapter 12: "*But ye are come to the blood of sprinkling that speaketh better things than that of Abel*".[6] I suggest the expression "the blood of sprinkling" means "the blood *for* sprinkling"; it is there to be applied to specific sins or situations where we have been at fault – that is ever

---

[6]Hebrews 12:24.

the sense in which the Bible uses the term. What a beautiful contrast between the blood of Abel ("the voice of thy brother's blood crieth unto Me from the ground")[7] and the blood of Jesus Christ.

> *Abel's blood for vengence,*
> *Pleaded to the skies,*
> *But the blood of Jesus*
> *For our pardon cries.*
>
> *Oft as it is sprinkled*
> *On our guilty hearts,*
> *Satan in confusion*
> *Terror-struck departs.*

It is sometimes complained that preachers do not preach the blood today. That may or may not be true, but the more important thing for us is not are we or they preaching the blood, but are we applying the blood to ourselves?

The second reference is also in Hebrews: "Having, therefore, brethren boldness to enter the holiest by the blood of Jesus … let us draw near … *having our hearts sprinkled from an evil conscience*".[8] Here we are told that it is the conscience on which the blood is to be sprinkled. As we have just said, how inexorable the faculty called conscience is. Nothing seems to pacify it once it is defiled – except the blood. In this verse it is described as a part of the heart. Indeed, we could say it is the heart of the heart, for if the

---

[7]Genesis 4:10.   [8]Hebrews 10:19, 22.

conscience is not at peace, the whole heart is not at peace either. But if the conscience is clean, the whole man is clean too. Therefore we must sprinkle, that is apply, the blood right there on the conscience. How? By repentance and faith – a definite clear cut repentance with regard to that of which it is accused, followed by an equally clear cut faith in the blood, as it is written, "a propitiation through faith in His blood."[9] Then you will know again "peace through the blood of His cross".[1]

Note that the phrase about the heart being sprinkled from an evil conscience is followed by the phrase, "and our bodies washed with pure water", the body meaning the outer life. When the blood has cleansed the conscience (the inner life), things will sometimes need to be put right in the outer life; apologies and restitution made, things stolen restored, necessary adjustments in all sorts of things made, whatever God may lead us to.

Peter in his first epistle has the third reference to sprinkling. "Elect according to the foreknowledge of God the Father, through sanctification of the Spirit, *unto obedience and sprinkling of the blood of Jesus* Christ."[2] I think that the grammatical construction of "obedience and sprinkling" is meant to indicate, "unto obedient sprinkling of the blood of Jesus Christ". To sprinkle the blood on the doorposts was an act of obedience on the part of the Israelites; God commanded them to do it. For us to sprinkle the blood of Jesus Christ on sin is an act of obedience, too.

---

[9]Romans 3:25.   [1]Colossians 1:20.   [2]1 Peter 1:2.

An obedient Christian is one who is quick to obey the Spirit's prompting as often as he is aware of sin.

Very often we are told that the essence of a victorious life is obedience. I am always left guessing as to what that really means. Do I make a blanket promise of obedience for the future? Or is it that I am facing a situation where I am not willing to take a right action, and at last I consent to go and do it?

That would be obedience, but far more helpful is this concept, that when the Spirit convicts me of wrong, I obey and apply the blood.

This helps me with regard to the many moral injunctions of the New Testament. How do I fit them in with the message of grace? When a certain moral injunction stands out and hits me, it is probably because that is the very point where I have done the thing forbidden, or failed to do the thing commanded. In that case, the first step of obedience is for me to repent and then sprinkle the blood upon it, or as we would say today, "put it under the blood". If, however, a moral injunction does not find me at fault, there is no call for action. But if and when it does find me falling short, this moral injunction is not a call for a new promise for the future, or new self-effort for the present, but a call to repent first and foremost, and that means the blood; and after that, restitution or apology to others, where necessary. So often, then, the first step of obedience is to sprinkle (or, apply) the blood of Jesus Christ.

The purpose of our election by God the Father and the working of the sanctifying Holy Spirit is all to "obedient sprinkling of the blood of Jesus Christ", that we might be obedient blood-sprinkling Christians.

Be of good courage, then, the moral injunctions often associated with grace are not appeals to the flesh to try to do better, which attempts the New Testament tells us are doomed to failure,[3] but are addressed to men in whom is the full potential to do all that is commanded, for Christ Himself is in them.

Three expressions

We are now in a position to look again at the three expressions to which we made reference earlier, the death of Christ, the cross of Christ, and the blood of Christ.

We said that these are not interchangeable terms, but that they each express a different aspect of truth and God does not use them indiscriminately.

First, there is the *death of Christ,* as for instance, in the verse "reconciled to God by the death of His Son".[4] This recounts that the Second Person of the Trinity became subject to mortal death "that through death He might destroy him that had the power of death, that is the devil, and deliver those who through fear of death were all their lifetime subject to bondage."[5]

Then there is the *cross of Christ* as in the passage, "He became obedient unto death, even the death of the cross."[6] It was not just to death that he humbled

---

[3]Romans 7:17–20 and Romans 8:6.   [4]Romans 5:10.
[5]Hebrews 2:14,15.   [6]Philippians 2:5–8.

Himself, but to a certain form of death, that of the cross. Death on the cross was reserved by the Romans for criminals, and the Jews only crucified those who were accursed of God, but in their case they called it a tree to fit in with their Scriptures.[7] But whichever it is called, it was for Him a disgrace, a matter of shame. It is the greatest epic of brokenness we know, only it is God's brokenness, not ours. The brokenness of the Deity is always designed to provoke the brokenness of the creature and induce him to take the sinner's place and find mercy.

The *blood of Christ is* different. His blood was only actually shed after He had said, "It is finished", and had dismissed His spirit. It was then that the Roman soldier pierced His side and there came out blood and water. That blood was a token, as we have seen, the judgment had been met and the work of redemption finished.[8] By its power the weakest saint is brought "clean over Jordan" into the fulness. It is, therefore, a joyous, victorious message and brings rest and release from striving to the seeker.

It is interesting to contrast the hymns about the cross and the hymns about the blood of Jesus. The first are solemn hymns, and rightly so, for they celebrate the brokenness of the Deity for us. The hymns about the blood are usually joyous, rhythmic hymns, sometimes it might almost be thought irreverently so. But they are right, for they are celebrating the triumph His blood brings to the sinner.

---

[7]Deuteronomy 21:22, 23 and Galatians 3:13.
[8]Exodus 12:13 and John 19:30.

A danger

Is there not a danger, you may say, that in extolling the blood and its power so much we might exalt it to become almost the fourth person of the Trinity – Father, Son, Holy Spirit and the Blood? Yes, there is that danger; but it is ever the blood *of Jesus*. It is the fact that it is His blood that makes it precious to us and gives it its power with God on behalf of sinners. We must guard against giving any other impression. Yet it is more Jesus than His cross is. The cross on which He died was exterior to Him, not a part of Him. But the blood was a part of Him. When He poured out His blood, He poured out His life, for "the life of the flesh is in the blood".[9] So when we talk about the blood, we are talking about Him, praise His dear Name!

---

[9]Leviticus 17:11

"Who is a God like unto Thee, that pardoneth iniquity, and passeth by the transgression of the remnant of His heritage? He retaineth not His anger for ever, because He delighteth in mercy" (Micah 7:18).

"In whom we have redemption through His blood, the forgiveness of sins, according to the riches of His grace" (Ephesians 1:7).

"And be ye kind one to another, tenderhearted, forgiving one another, even as God for Christ's sake hath forgiven you" (Ephesians 4:32).

6

FORGIVENESS
for the guilty

A Christian who was offered by a friend of mine a cassette on which was recorded this message on forgiveness, replied, "I think I know all about the Bible teaching on forgiveness; it is one of the more elementary truths with which I am familiar".

My friend replied, "Did you know that forgiving and foregoing are always linked; and that to forgive us sinners God had to forego His claims against us and suffer the loss Himself? Did you know that the same holds good for us: and to forgive someone the wrongs he has perpetrated against us, we have to forego any claims we have against him and suffer the loss ourselves? Did you know that?"

"No", he replied, "I don't think I really did."

You, too, might well have to say, "I don't think I knew that forgiving and foregoing are linked". Neither did I until recently. I can trust that by approaching the subject from this angle, it will light up the whole glorious theme of forgiveness, not only to your blessing, but to the blessing of the others you may find you have to forgive.

Forgiving and foregoing

God's forgiveness of us is intended to lead us to forgive others. In place after place in the New Testament, the forgiven are constantly urged to forgive. I have set out in the footnotes an array of texts from the gospels and the epistles, which teach this.[1] It is probably the injunction that is repeated more frequently and insistently than any other in the New Testament, and it has a prominent place in the Lord's Prayer. Indeed, in some places our forgiving of another is to be taken as an indication as to whether we ourselves are forgiven. If we display an unforgiving spirit we bring into doubt our whole relationship to God.[2]

An unforgiving spirit will tear us apart pyschologically, and sometimes physically, too. A medical consultant I knew would sometimes ask patients with certain symptoms, "Whom are you hating?" On the spiritual front the effect of unforgiveness can spell the death of all hopes of revival. You may not have done the initial wrong yourself in a situation, but you have reacted wrongly to the one who has, and that can make you as wrong as the other – until you forgive.

A new sinology

Inasmuch as it is sin that is being forgiven, we shall

---

[1] Matthew 6:12–15 and 18:32–35, Mark 11:25, Luke 11:4, Ephesians 4:32, Colossians 3:13. [2] Matthew 18:35, Mark 11:26.

need a new understanding of what sin is, for it is just here that we may be hazy. Many of us need, perhaps, a new sinology. In offering this definition of sin, culled deep from the Word of God, I want to be as careful as I can in setting it out, clause by clause. It could make all the difference to our experience of God's forgiveness of us and of our forgiving one another.

First, our sins are not merely mistakes, or even insignificant misdeeds, but are *personal wrongs against God,* the moral Ruler of the universe. Though it would seem that most of our sins are against our fellows, we have sinned most of all against God. It is His will we have despised, and His commandments we have broken. We need to confess with David, "Against Thee only have I sinned and done this evil in Thy sight."[3]

Second, in the wrongs which we have perpetrated against Him, *God has suffered grave loss.* It was certainly so in the case of David's sin. Nathan the prophet was sent to him to make clear that what he had done was against the backdrop of the goodness and generosity of God. He recites to David how God had anointed him king while but a shepherd boy, how He had delivered him out of the hand of Saul and given him his master's household, and also the house of Israel and Judah to rule over. The message continues, "If that had been too little, I would moreover have given unto thee such and such things. Wherefore hast thou despised the commandment of

---

[3]Psalm 51:4.

Jehovah to do evil in His sight?"[4] In other words, it was as if God had said to him, "When so much was given to you, why must you snatch at the one small fruit that was denied you – another man's wife – as if I was not willing to give you yet more, as if I did not know what was best designed for your happiness, as if I did not love you?" There seems to be grief in those words, for in them stands revealed all the deep hurt and loss that God had suffered through David's sin.

Our sins, too, whatever they may be, attitudes as well as actions, have also been committed against the same backdrop of God's goodness and generosity and have inflicted grievous hurt upon Him. Others may have suffered loss at our hands, but none more so than God Himself.

That in turn means that because of the loss He has sustained *God has a claim on the sinner for reparation.* It is a built-in law of life that if I damage another man's property he has a claim on me to make it good. How much more, then, has God a claim for reparation. In spite of His compassions, justice demands it. The sinner may not always know what he should do by way of reparation, but his conscience tells him that God has this claim against him; "God requireth that which is past".[5] There is coming a day, the judgment day, when those reparations are due to be met.

This brings us to something which shows the plight of the sinner to be even more desperate. *This*

---

[4]2 Samuel 12:7–9.   [5]Ecclesiastes 3:15.

claim for reparation is one he is unable to meet; he has nothing to pay. He will not be able to make adequate reparation in that final time, nor can he make it in the present time. His attempts at righteousness and religion are not legal tender in heaven. If he were able to live from today a perfect Christian life that might balance the books for today, but what about the wrongs of former days? The sinner has a debt he cannot pay, and a sense of guilt he cannot shake off. Interestingly, in German debt and guilt are the same word, *Schuld.* Because the sinner has nothing to pay, he faces eternal ruin.

> *Nothing to pay! Ah nothing to pay!*
> *Never a word of excuse to say!*
> *Year after year thou hast filled the score,*
> *Owing thy Lord still more and more.*

There, then, is our definition of sin, describing the plight which the sinner is in before God. The importance of this definition is that it gives us the background and the whole scenario of the divine forgiveness of the sinner. If all that we have said about the grace of God is true, then the sinner's plight is the perfect foil for that grace.

> *O loving wisdom of our God,*
> *When all was sin and shame,*
> *A second Adam to the fight,*
> *And to the rescue came.*

Magnanimity of God

In the light of the definition just given, we can see what the divine forgiveness is. It is nothing less than God deciding to do the vastly magnanimous thing of foregoing His just claim for reparation and loosing man from his debt of sin. Little wonder such forgiveness is accompanied by joy and relief in the one forgiven. Even in earthly affairs nothing burdens a man so much as his unpaid debts. He sighs over the fact that he is always behind with them and never seems to be able to catch up with them. What an unspeakable relief to such a man if he were to know that somehow or other all those accounts had been cancelled or settled. How much more is there joy unspeakable when a man knows God has deliberately given up His claim against him and loosed him from his debt of sin!

I call this a vastly magnanimous thing for God to do, because God cannot forego His claim against us without suffering the loss Himself. If, for instance, I were to forego my claim against a man who owed me £1,000 and forgave him that debt, because, say, he was deeply embarrassed at not being able to pay me and it was spoiling our friendship, I would lose £1,000. I might feel that I could not afford to lose that amount, but if I am to forgive him that debt so that he can be at ease with me in the future, there is nothing for it, I have to be willing to be out of pocket.

So it is with God. If He foregoes His claim for reparation against us in order to forgive our debt,

He will have to suffer the loss Himself. He gave His Son to die, the Just for the unjust, to settle that debt of sin. He had to do it that way, in order that justice might be done and be seen to be done. "Through one act of righteousness the free gift came unto all men to justification of life."[6] The judgment-bearing of the Lord Jesus on the cross is in Romans chapter five regarded as the great act of righteousness of the second Adam bringing justification to all that believe, in contrast to the offence of the first Adam by which judgment came on all to condemnation.

More than that, in actually dispensing His forgiveness, He is letting the various issues in question go, being willing to be treated in the way we have treated Him.

Without such willingness there would be no forgiveness for us.

There is no question, however, of Jesus having to suffer the loss again for each act of pardoning grace. He has already suffered the whole loss in an all-inclusive way and it is finished. There is nothing more for Him to do, or suffer, or for you to do either; the loss has already been met. There is no need even for you to plead for His forgiveness. You will get it if you simply fulfil the condition, "If we confess our sins …". This follows the words, "If we say that we have no sin …"; the confessing of our sins is in contrast to the justifying of ourselves, saying we have no sin. To confess that we were wrong, where before we had said we were right, is very humbling,

---

[6]Romans 5:18.

especially when we have to say it to another Person, even Jesus. But that is all; His forgiveness is yours at that moment. Indeed, you can regard it as something already achieved and available for you. But never forget that His forgiving and His foregoing are for ever linked.

He paid a debt He did not owe;
I owed a debt I could not pay,
I needed Someone to take, to take my guilt away
But now I sing a brand new song,
Amazing grace how sweet the sound;
Christ Jesus paid the debt that I could never pay.

Magnanimity is derived from two Latin words which together means large-heartedness. When applied to the Deity, it is another word for grace, but fills it out, presenting our Jehovah God as Mr Greatheart. We must not think of Jesus being that and God the Father as being something else. It is God the Father who is Mr Greatheart supremely because He sent Jesus. Only such a One would have done that for a world undone. Thank you, God, for sending Jesus.

Forgiving king

Jesus told a parable of an unforgiving servant.[7] It is in two parts, and it is only the second part that deals with the unforgiving servant. The first part could

---

[7]Matthew 18:23–35.

well be called the parable of "the forgiving king".

It begins with the servant who is discovered to be in debt to his king to the tune of 10,000 talents. We are not told how he managed to contract such a debt, but we are not surprised to learn that he had "nothing wherewith to pay". This exactly parallels the sinner's position of being bankrupt before God.

The king "commanded him to be sold and his wife, and his children, and payment to be made." It was a terrible thing to do, to split that family and sell them as slaves to various households, but the law permitted it. This pictures God's first option, to banish the sinner into outer darkness for ever. If He did so, no angel could charge Him with injustice, for this is what we deserve.

The servant, alarmed at such a prospect, suggested an alternative. "Lord, have patience with me, and I will pay thee all." What he meant was, if the king would give him time, he would pay so much a week out of his wages until the whole debt was cleared. It was naïve of him to make such a suggestion, for he would have to live a long life to pay off such a debt, but it was born out of desperation. This pictures the sort of bargain we would like to make with God, that if He will give us time, we will improve and be good Christians in the future, doing our best to honour Him, and in that way we will ultimately pay off our debt. But the debt of falling short is too vast; the whole of the New Testament declares that by works shall no man be justified in God's sight.[8]

---

[8]Romans 3:20.

A magnanimous third option came into the king's heart. He was moved with compassion at the plight of that man and his family. He decided to forego his just claim against him and forgive him the debt, even though it meant suffering the loss himself. The man could hardly believe his ears at the gracious proposition of the king. This is God's third option, the option of grace – to forego His claim on the sinner, suffer the loss Himself in the Person of His Son on Calvary and forgive the sinner.

The king would have to sustain a considerable loss to forgive that servant for he would have to make the money good to his exchequer. Years ago an African preacher with whom I was travelling, William Nagenda, a beloved revival leader, added a short word after I had finished speaking on this parable. He imagined that servant later going past the palace and seeing a van drawn up outside. It was being loaded with priceless treasures out of the king's palace, to be taken down to the city auction rooms for sale.

When the servant asked the king why this was happening, he replied, "It is to reimburse the exchequer for the sum I forgave you."

"But why is so much being taken?"

The reply was, "It was a bigger sum than any of us expected."

That African added this comment quite spontaneously, because he had caught a sight of the ineffable loss God in Jesus Christ had suffered in order to forgive him and us, and he wanted us all to see that it was a bigger debt than we thought.

Unforgiving servant

In the second part of the parable we have the story of the unforgiving servant, in marked contrast to the forgiving king. "But the same servant (that is the one who had been so abundantly forgiven) went out and found one of his fellow-servants, which owed him a hundred denarii (a comparatively trivial amount): and he laid hands on him, and took him by the throat, saying, Pay me that thou owest. And his fellow-servant fell down at his feet and besought him, saying, Have patience with me and I will pay thee all (exactly the same words as the first servant had used to the king, but with what different response!); and he would not: but went and cast him into prison till he should pay the debt."[9]

They each had a creditor and they were both suffering loss and embarrassment as a result of the debts. The king certainly suffered embarrassment as a result of the huge sum by which his budget was short. Although in the case of the servant the sum owing to him was small, he was none the less short by that amount, and with his modest standard of living he and his wife would have felt it. They both knew they had a legal claim for reparation and were prepared to take action.

There was one big way in which they differed. The king forgave his servant his debt, though it ran into millions, and set him free, whereas the

---

[9]Matthew 18:30.

very same servant refused to forgive his creditor his debt, though it was by comparison insignificant. He put him in court and from there into prison.

Can we identify?

Before we enquire what was the reason for this big difference, and seek to learn from it, let us see if we can identify with the unforgiving servant, for he takes the centre of the stage at this point. It may be we shall discover quite a bit about ourselves.

There is not one of us who at one time or another has not been wronged, or insulted, or ill-used by others. There are, as a result, those people who are our creditors; they owe us an apology at the very least, perhaps much more than that. Perhaps there is not much likelihood of their paying that debt. So we feel they are still our creditors; they have done nothing to put things right, and we have not forgiven them for what they have done.

Then, too, we have suffered loss as a result of their words and actions, at the very least we have felt hurt. We have carried with us that sense of hurt, perhaps for years.

As a result, we feel we have a claim on them for some sort of reparation. We may not be sure what we expect them to do, but the fact that they make no movement in that direction makes our feelings all the stronger.

We certainly have not forgiven them and if not to forgive another is to put oneself out of fellowship with God, then we are out of fellowship with God. If to harbour unforgiveness, resentment and bitterness is to produce harmful psychological results in us, then to that extent we are not happy Christians.

This lead me ask, why have you not forgiven that other person? You might say, he (or she) owes so much, has caused me so much hurt. Then, I must ask another question: why would the servant in the parable refuse to forgive so little a debt when the king forgave so great a one?

Why have you not forgiven?

To forgive from the heart is sometimes hard. Even when you know you ought to, and when you even want to, it is still hard. Why did the servant find it hard, and why do you? The answer comes out in this parable. You have been unwilling to forego your claim for reparation and suffer the loss yourself. It was like this with the servant. It is utterly impossible to forgive a wrong without being willing to suffer the loss occasioned by that wrong. Deity could not do it, and neither can you. His love for us was equal to it, but our love for the other person is not.

At bottom, pride and a standing up for our rights are the reasons for the unforgiving spirit which has spoilt our fellowship with God. "It is not right; it is not fair", we say. "It should not have been done to me." Sometimes we feel that to forgive a wrong as freely as that is to condone the behaviour. Rightly understood, it does not mean that at all. It simply means that you are willing to bear it. God will give you all the help you need to do so.

Forgiveness is God acting at His greatest because of the loss He is willing to sustain. That is why we sing, "Who is a pardoning God like Thee, or who has grace so rich and free?" You are never so godlike as when you are forgiving another.

Forgiving without repentance

This is a hard path to walk in some circumstances, especially if you feel that if there were repentance and apology on the other side, it would make forgiveness on your part much easier. But you must forgive nonetheless, or else suffer the spiritual loss that so often comes with an unforgiving spirit. The relationship cannot be fully healed unless there is repentance on the other side, but even if there is no repentance, the surrender of your rights to God must be complete so that your forgiveness becomes available.

To illustrate, I recall the story of a godly African working and living on a tea plantation in Uganda. Another African, working on the same plantation, but not a Christian, seduced his wife, who went to live with him. What made things specially difficult for the one who had lost his wife was that he had to go to work every day past the house where his wife was living with the other man. The Christian's friends gave him their love, prayer and fellowship, and God wonderfully helped him to bear this grievous wrong. Some time later a special wind of the Spirit began to blow – by that I mean a time of revival – when many were convicted of sin and turned their lives over to Christ. The man who seduced the woman was amongst one of them. One of the first things he did after he was saved was to seek out the man whom he had wronged so grievously, and beg his forgiveness. To this the other replied, "There is nothing to forgive; I forgave you the day you took her from me."

The day the other man took her from him he consented to suffer the loss in order to be able to forgive him. It was doubtless a struggle to take that stance at first, but he came right through to make the necessary surrender, so that when at last the other sinner in the situation repented, it was to find that forgiveness was already available.

It is a picture in miniature of the divine forgiveness of sinners, and the way in which grace makes it available for them. The whole relationship with the other person is not restored until he repents, and not even Calvary restores man's relationship to God until he repents. Some who have never realised before that forgiving is so deeply linked with foregoing just cannot face it. If you should feel like that, confess it to Jesus. Do not try to make yourself willing, or even ask God that you might be made so, but rather confess that you are not willing, and come to the cross again. Jesus will forgive you for not forgiving and bring you into rest and help you in the situation.

Where this is not done

Where an individual does not do this, but insists on harbouring an unforgiving spirit, he only succeeds in tearing himself apart and inflicting severe psychological damage on himself and ends up of no use to God or man.

I used to think my relationship to God could be, described as a two-point circuit, God and me, which I had only to ensure was not broken and I would be in fellowship with God. But I have since discovered that it is a three-point one; God, me and my fellow, and the divine electricity has to go round three points rather than two. I may imagine there is nothing wrong between me and God, but if things are not right between me and another the circuit is as much broken as if the break was more directly between me and God. There is no way round it, but you must forgive the wrong you have suffered, or forego the blessedness of the flow of the divine electricity. The other may not respond to your change of attitude, and you need not condemn yourself on that account; the electricity will flow again as far as you are concerned.

Keeping forgiveness up to date

A gracious attitude to others and a readiness to forgive them their faults is simply the outflow of a fresh experience of the divine forgiveness.

It is essential, therefore, that we keep the forgiveness of our own sins up to date.

Years ago I met an unusual woman in the deep

south of the United States on one of my trips. She was well into her 90's and had been for years a missionary in China, during which time she had been involved in what has become known as the Shantung revival. According to the rules of her missionary society, she had to retire and come home at 65, which she did, albeit reluctantly. Then she started another career, that of a Bible teacher with regard to revival, of which she had had such a rich experience. She was always talking about "keeping her sins forgiven up to date." When she was interviewed for a magazine article about her experience under the Communists in China, and how she coped, she had only one answer, "I just kept my sins forgiven up to date." When asked what she did when the Communists came on to her station and tried to get access to her girls' school, she again replied, "I just kept my sins forgiven up to date."

It might sound a rather quaint way of putting it, but it was very deep, for one can imagine how a woman in her situations would have had reactions of fear, resentment and anger. She called them sin and kept them forgiven up to date. It was not merely keeping her sins confessed up to date, but, better, forgiven up to date, right into peace and victory. That meant she had a sight of the power of the blood of Jesus such as we all need. That, then, was all she had to say, and it worked, or rather, Jesus did.

If in this way our experience of forgiveness is fresh, our love for others will be fresh, too. But when forgiveness is old, love becomes cold; and we become hard and unforgiving again.

Sending away sin

I have not yet given the real essential meaning of the word "forgiveness," and I want to do that as we conclude this chapter. There are four different Greek words translated "forgive," or "forgiveness," in the New Testament, all of them with their slightly different emphasis. The one most frequently used, indeed the standard word for forgive, or forgiveness, is *aphiemi,* which occurs no less than 64 times. It means, "to send away". This gives the forgiveness of sin its real meaning which is "sin sent away", the matchless act of a pardoning God.

As you might expect, this meaning of *aphiemi,* "the sending away of sin" is reflected in the ritual offerings given by Moses in the Book of Leviticus. No ritual is more moving and more obviously a type of Christ than that of the Scapegoat, which was performed on the annual Day of Atonement, described in Leviticus chapter 16. On that day atonement was made, not only for the nation's sins, but also for the tabernacle itself, God's sanctuary in their midst. It had been defiled by being used by the priests, and atoning blood had to be sprinkled on it.

Two goats were chosen, one for the Lord so that its blood could be sprinkled on the altar, and the other to be the scapegoat for the people. "And Aaron shall lay both his hands upon the head of the live goat, and confess over him all the iniquities of the children of Israel, and all their transgressions in all their sins, putting them upon the head of the goat, and shall send him away by the hand of a fit man into the wilderness; and the goat shall bear upon him all their iniquities unto a land not inhabited: and he shall let go the goat in the wilderness."[1] It does not need much insight to understand that it is meant to symbolise the "sending away" of our sins, their memory, their accusation and shame, borne away by Christ "into a land not inhabited", the forgetfulness of eternity.

Holman Hunt, the great Victorian painter of the Pre-Raphaelite school, whose picture of Christ knocking at the door, the Light of the World, most people know, also painted a picture of the scapegoat. He went to the Holy Land and spent months in the wilderness of Judea, painting in great detail the wilderness with the lonely scapegoat wandering "unto a land not inhabited".

It must have been a great surprise to the wealthy, fashionable crowd who came to that year's Royal Academy in London to gaze upon a huge painting of "The Scapegoat", and underneath the frame the text, "… and the goat shall bear upon him all their iniquities unto a land not inhabited." The people were gazing upon God's solemn way of "sending away" their sins, doing it in the person of His Son as their Scapegoat, not as something apart from Himself, but "His own self in His own body". Thus God sent our sins away, really away, never to be seen again. As the hymn writer wrote, "Buried, He carried my sins far away."

Dear troubled one, believe it and be free!

---

[1] Leviticus 16:21, 22.

"How much more shall the blood of Christ cleanse your conscience from dead works to serve the living God" (Hebrews 9:14).

"God is light, and in Him is no darkness at all. If we say that we have fellowship with Him and walk in darkness, we lie, and do not the truth: but if we walk in the light, as He is in the light, we have fellowship one with another and *the blood of Jesus Christ His Son cleanseth us from all sin.* But if we say that we have no sin, we deceive ourselves, and the truth is not in us. If we confess our sins He is faithful and just to forgive us our sins and to *cleanse us from all unrighteousness* (1 John 1:5–9).

7

CLEANSING
for the defiled

Sin not only renders us guilty before God, but leaves us defiled on the inside. Here our great need is for cleansing, and this is another element of the good news for bad people. Paul in his first letter to the Corinthians enumerates those who shall not inherit the kingdom of God, and gives a positively horrendous list of sinners and their sins. Then he adds the glorious words, "and such were some of you: but ye are washed, but ye are sanctified, but ye are justified".[1] I especially emphasise the word washed, because that is now our theme. In applying ourselves to this, we must have in the forefront of our mind the great foundational passage on cleansing in the first chapter of the first epistle of John which is printed on the page opposite.[2]

Its relevance lies in the fact that "if we confess our sins", two things are promised, forgiveness of our sins and cleansing from all unrighteousness. We have dealt with divine forgiveness in the previous chapter and now we come to divine cleansing, and

---

[1] 1 Corinthians 6:11.   [2] 1 John 1:5–9.

my purpose is that we should make sure we have experienced both of them.

These two terms are not synonomous and it is only too possible, as we shall see, to experience one without the other, to know forgiveness without cleansing, though it was never intended by God that they should be separated.

Forgiveness and cleansing

It was the necessity of distinguishing between forgiveness and cleansing that led me in the first place to give the whole series of messages on the Great Words of the Gospel. I was finding that among Christians the words were often used indiscriminately, as if they meant the same thing. This was especially true amongst those of my brothers who had begun a new "walk in the light as He is the light". Such were, quite rightly, ready to share their experience with others and in doing so would often speak of being cleansed from this or that sin. As I listened and was blessed through their testimonies, I nonetheless sometimes wondered if they should not have spoken of being forgiven this or that.

Forgiveness is something objective and happens outside of us, in the records before God where He now assures the debt is cleared. Cleansing is subjective and is something that happens within us as a conscious experience.

Cleansing of the conscience

What is the particular part of us that is to be cleansed? Is it the thoughts that need to be cleansed, or the affections, or the memory? None of these things, firstly. Scripture speaks supremely of the conscience needing to be cleansed. This is abundantly clear in the verse in Hebrews we have already quoted in a previous chapter, "How much more shall the blood of Christ cleanse your conscience from dead works to serve the living God."[3] There are other verses, too, that point to the conscience as the crucial factor in the human make-up.

I would define conscience as the God-given faculty in every man that approves of him when he does right and disapproves of him when he does wrong. Inasmuch as the basic thing about all of us is that we are sinners, we get far more disapproval from our consciences than approval. This means that often our consciences are defiled with what the hymn writers speak of as "the stain of sin".

Also in the epistle of Hebrews we have the phrase, "having our hearts sprinkled from an evil conscience".[4] The part of the heart that gets cleansed is, apparently, the conscience. Indeed, the conscience is the heart of the heart. When the conscience is cleansed, the whole heart is cleansed, and a man is said to have a pure heart. But while the conscience remains defiled, the whole man is defiled. This,

---

[3]Hebrews 9:14.   [4]Hebrews 10:22.

then, is where the blood of Jesus Christ has to be applied.

What an extraordinary faculty this thing called conscience is! When it is defiled, it can make us miserable in heart, unwell in body, ill at ease with our fellows, and certainly make us feel cut off from God. There are differences in sensitivity of conscience between one man and another, as there are differences in scales. Some scales are designed to weigh the largest bulks and will not register anything less than a hundredweight; on the other hand, there are scales in our laboratories so sensitive that they will register the weight of a postage stamp, or much less. In a similar way, some people's consciences register only when they have got themselves involved with the police; there are others for whom the least omission registers as guilt. It might be regarded as a questionable blessing to have a conscience as sensitive at that, but unless we have a conscience sensitised and instructed by the Holy Spirit, how are we to know what has gone wrong and where to get right? Charles Wesley wrote:

> *I want a principle within*
> *Of jealous, godly fear;*
> *A sensibility of sin,*
> *A pain to feel it near.*

> *O may the least omission pain*
> *My well-instructed soul;*
> *And drive me to the blood again,*
> *That makes the wounded whole.*

The passage of time does nothing to remove the stains of sin from the conscience. Long after sin has ceased to occupy the thoughts, and long after it has ceased to grip the heart, and even when it has almost faded from the memory, the stain of it remains upon the conscience, giving the soul a sense of unease. It is rather like the stains in a cup a person has failed to wash before going to bed. In the morning the cup is certainly empty of the coffee which was drunk the previous evening, but the stains remain. Left for weeks the stains still remain. Even so the defilement on the conscience abides long after the sin has ceased. Indeed, in view of its on-going legacy, it has not ceased at all; it is still active in accusing our consciences. It demands to see divine justice satisfied if it is to be pacified. But how?

That is precisely what the blood of Jesus demonstrates. As we have seen, it is a token of judgment met at the cross, of the fire of God's wrath burnt out, of which nothing is left but the ashes. The great work of judgment-bearing that Jesus did for us ought to be sufficient for the most sensitive of consciences, as it is for God, and a penitent has got to believe it and accept peace with God through its power. All this can be his on the simple confession: "if we confess our sins", a confession that pleads no extenuating circumstances nor blames another, but goes into the witness box against itself. Then the conscience is fully cleansed by the blood of Jesus and we are able to serve the living God with joy and liberty.

There is the possibility, then, of knowing

ourselves forgiven, and yet to continue with a heart that is still condemning us, and to be dogged with a sense of being wrong on particular matters, large or small, or just oppressed overall. All this we can lose in the "fountain open for sin and uncleanness" and we can walk off in freedom.

Whiter than snow

In a previous chapter we considered that great penitential prayer of David's in Psalm 51; "Wash me and I shall be whiter than snow."[5]

What do you think it means for your heart and conscience to be made, not as white as snow, but whiter than snow? It takes some thinking of, and certainly some believing, to comprehend such excess of cleansing. I can only imagine that it means a heart that no longer condemns itself, and no longer has any self-recrimination, that no longer takes a stick to itself, that is no longer dogged with a sense of not being good enough. Of course it is not good enough, but we don't have to mourn over that fact – we can be set free from all the accusations of it. We are accepted by God wholly and solely on the ground of the blood of Jesus. Make your personal list of what it means to be made whiter than snow, and then dare to believe that that is what the blood of Jesus effects between you and God.

This is something that does not happen merely automatically and unconsciously; we have to extend

---

[5]Psalm 51:7.

our faith to it quite definitely, having first confessed our need. The Epistle to the Romans says that Jesus is "set forth to be a propitiation through faith in His blood". Read into that word "propitiation" all the grounds on which you hope to be whiter than snow, and then exercise your faith in that blood to that end, and give praise to God.

> *Lord Jesus, for this I most humbly intreat,*
> *I wait, blessed Lord, at Thy crucified feet;*
> *By faith for my cleansing I see Thy blood flow,*
> *Now wash me and I shall be whiter than snow.*

Dead works

In the verse of which we have made so much, Hebrews 9:14, it does not say that the blood of Christ cleanses the conscience merely from sin, (as we have seen, it does do that), but it says it cleanses the conscience from dead works. They are not the same as sin, but they certainly oppress the conscience as much, and we need desperately to have our consciences cleansed from them.

The New Testament speaks of three sorts of works. There are wicked works. It is not difficult for us to know what they are, straight forward, down-the-line sin, as normally understood. There are good works; these are not random good deeds, but rather, "good works that God hath before ordained that we should walk in them",[6] those

---

[6]Ephesians 2:10.

spheres of service for Himself and others that He has planned for us. Then there are dead works,[7] something between wicked works and good works.

Dead works are the things we feel we ought to do to become better Christians, but which we have never succeeded in doing. It would be interesting to pass around a group of Christians a sheet of paper for each to write down the things he thinks he ought to do to become a better Christian and to be more used of God. What would we find on such a list? Perhaps that we ought to give ourselves more to prayer, that we ought to have more faith and confidence in God, that we ought to spend more time reading our Bibles, that we ought to be more caring for others, that we ought to manifest more holiness and patience, that we ought to have greater readiness to bear witness. The list could go on – ought, ought, ought.

If we try seriously to put these things into practice, we find ourselves facing a problem – we never quite succeed in doing them. There is nothing wrong with the standards that we espouse – "the commandment is holy and just and good"[8] – but the trouble is that we seem unable to achieve them.

What an impasse we are in! We know what we ought to do to make us better Christians, and we try, but are never able to do them, at least not as we should. The result is that our failure to do these things only burdens our consciences and we end up with a greater sense of condemnation than before.

---

[7]Hebrews 9:14.   [8]Romans 7:12.

So it is, many Christians are going round with consciences burdened by the prayers they have not prayed, the promises they have not kept, the souls they have not witnessed to, and so on. The attempt to do these things is so often dead and heavy, with no breath of the Spirit about them; while the failure to do them is deadlier still, for they only add to the sense of condemnation.

These, I suggest, are what is meant by dead works; these are what burden the conscience; these take from us our liberty in service. As I repent of my sins Jesus brings me by His blood into that fellowship with God for which I have been struggling. What I was attempting to find by my works, I receive as a gift at the foot of the cross.

If you lost a ten pound note or a ten dollar bill, and were looking everywhere for it, what would be the first thing you would do when you found it? You would stop looking for it! The first thing I do when I have found peace and fulness at the foot of the cross is to stop looking for it in other ways. This is freedom indeed. It was this that Bunyan was referring to when he described in Pilgrim's Progress a burden rolling off Pilgrim's back when he saw the cross. It was not merely the burden of sin that he lost that day, but also the burden of dead works. It was this cleansing the conscience from dead works that Jesus was referring to when He said, "Come unto Me, all ye that labour and are heavy laden, and I will give you rest."

This is so that we can serve the living God, "not in the oldness of the letter" as a legal obligation, but "in the newness of the Spirit",[9] as a glad act of love and gratitude to the One who has set us free.

Walk in the light

Both fellowship and cleansing in the blood of Jesus are conditional according to the Apostle John. "But if we walk in the light, as He is in the light, we have fellowship one with another and the blood of Jesus Christ, God's Son, cleanses us from all sin."[1] Light and darkness in John's writings are not vague synonyms for good and evil; light is that which reveals and darkness is that which hides. In this verse God is said to be the One who is light; that is, He shows up everything as it is. We are called upon to walk in the light as He is in the light, which means to agree with God that sin is what His light shows to be sin. If we do that we are promised that the blood of Jesus will cleanse us from all sin. This makes a walk in the light not something to be feared, but something to be welcomed, for what His light reveals, His blood cleanses. Furthermore, the reward of light received is more light, and for such new revelations the blood of Jesus is always more than enough.

---

[9]Romans 7:6.   [1]1 John 1:7.

Is conscience infallible?

Is conscience infallible? The answer is no. Just as a watch has to be checked and corrected by the time signal, so has conscience to be corrected and informed by the Word of God and the Spirit of God. Left to itself it can malfunction and bring you into bondage. It can, for instance, accuse you of not doing enough "works" to get God's blessings, when all the time God does not want you to get them by works at all, but by faith, as a gift.

Conscience can play strange tricks on us if it is not informed by the Word. An instance of this is the experience of Philip of Spain, who was sure that the failure of his Armada and other national undertakings was due to his not having put to death more Protestant heretics and he mourned before God over it! When conscience is taught and informed by grace, it is a happy ally to the Holy Spirit, who is ever the senior partner in the work of conviction. Its greatest work is, to use Charles Wesley's phrase, to

Drive me to the blood again,
That makes the wounded whole.

This is always at the instigation of the Holy Spirit. Bless His dear Name!

"Being justified by His grace as a gift through the redemption that is in Christ Jesus, whom God hath set forth to be a propitiation through faith in His blood, to declare His righteousness for the passing over of the sins done aforetime in the forebearance of God; to declare, I say, at this time His righteousness: that He might be just and the justifier of him that believeth in Jesus" (Romans 3:24–26).

"Now to him that worketh not, but believeth on Him that justifieth the ungodly, his faith is counted unto him for righteousness" (Romans 4:4).

"Now it was not written for his sake alone, that it was imputed, if we believe on Him that raised up Jesus our Lord from the dead; who was delivered for our offences, and was raised again for our justification" (Romans 4:23–25).

"Therefore we conclude that a man is justified by faith apart from the works of the law" (Romans 3:28).

"Ye see then how that by works a man is justified and not by faith only" (James 2:24).

8

JUSTIFICATION
for the ungodly

We come now to the great subject of God's justification of the sinner, or to use Paul's words, "God justifying the ungodly"[1] – one of the most exciting items
of the good news we are proclaiming. It was the
rediscovery of this truth that produced the
Reformation in the sixteenth century under Martin
Luther, Calvin, Zwingli, and the mighty eighteenth
century revival in England and America, under the
Wesleys, Whitefield, Jonathan Edwards and others.

It is usually referred to as "Justification by faith"
rather than only "Justification", because the basic
rediscovery consisted in the fact that sinners are
justified before God by faith and not by works. Paul
fought this battle long and hard with the Judaisers
and the legalists in his day. You can see the battle
line swaying through his epistles and in the story of
the Acts. But the victory was won and the Gospel
secured for us today. However, the Church since
then has again and again apostasised from this truth
in varying degrees, from grace to law and from faith

---

[1]Romans 4:5.

to works, and it has always meant her decline; in those situations she has become little more than a "valley full of dry bones."[2] But the rediscovery of this truth has always led to her revival, gloriously so, for it is an essential part of the revival experience. From this spring still flows the sweetest water for the souls of men.

If God justifies you

Instead of beginning with an ordered explanation of justification by faith, let me start with one of many personal applications to be derived from this truth to show at the very start that we are dealing with that which will move and bless our hearts, and not merely inform our minds.

I read somewhere, "the man who is justified by faith need not worry what people think of him." A good word indeed! This is based obviously on Paul's words, "It is God that justifieth! Who is he that condemneth?"[3] Paul's argument is if God justifies you and shows Himself on your side, it matters not who else accuses you. We all know we cannot go through life without being accused or criticised, and even if people are not criticising us right now, they might one day. Some of us are all the time tortured by what we fear people are thinking of us.

This is serious for it strikes at the basis of our security. If others think we are wrong, perhaps God does too, and we lose all confidence. Then we

---

[2]Ezekiel 1:37.   [3]Romans 8:33, 34.

develop a paranoia, and become quick to defend and justify ourselves, which only makes us more miserable.

But if it is God who justifies us, and gives unmistakable tokens that He does, who is he that condemns us? You need have no doubts that you are justified by faith – the whole epistle to the Romans was written that you might know you are. You may say, "What a blessed experience to have! What would I not give to be free from the diversion and preoccupation of worrying what others are thinking and saying of me?" Give nothing – such relief is yours gratuitously; it is one of the spin-offs of knowing yourself justified by faith.

A basic definition

God's justification of the sinner by faith is the very heart of the gospel. It says so in the opening verses of Paul's epistle to the Romans. "I am not ashamed of the gospel of Christ: for it is the power of God unto salvation to every one that believeth … for therein is the righteousness of God revealed, from faith to faith."[4]

I have begun by stating that justification by faith is the heart of the gospel, and then substantiated it by quoting this text, "for therein the righteousness of God is revealed." Thereafter in the epistle to the Romans the two words "righteousness" and "justification" always seem to appear together as if there is

---

[4]Romans 1:16, 17.

a close link between them. In fact, they are inter-
changable. They have the same root word in the
original Greek and mean the same; righteousness is
the noun and to justify is the verb. It is only the limi-
tations of the English language that has made the
translators use a noun and verb that sound so
dissimilar. To keep to the same root they ought to
have translated justify as "righteousify". Of course,
that is not a true English word, but it shows what
God does when he justifies a believing sinner – He
"righteousifies" him, that is, He imputes to him a
righteousness he does not otherwise possess.

How easy it is in ordinary affairs to impute to
another person unworthy motives, which are not
really there at all! Here is grace doing the opposite,
"God justifying the ungodly", that is, God imputing
to the self-confessed but believing sinner a righteousness that he does not otherwise possess. He
does not have any righteousness or attainments of
his own, but he does have some confidence in the
God of grace who deals mercifully with sinners
who turn to Him. God says to him, in effect, "Even
if you have nothing else to your credit, you have
faith as a grain of mustard seed that I have something good for sinners, that I justify the ungodly; so
I am going to count that feeble faith to you for a
righteousness, which is going to be entirely satis-
factory to Me."[5]

I need to define more precisely Paul's use of the
word righteousness because he uses it in a different

---

[5]Romans 4:6.

sense from the way in which we normally use the word.

Paul normally uses the word not of a man's personal righteousness of character, but of his right standing with God. A beloved Bible teacher in England in my younger days, the Rev. Guy King, in his notes on Romans consistently translated righteousness as normally understood. But if a man is not right with God, he is not right anywhere.

The first thing the gospel does is to tackle this, man's foundational need. It reveals and proffers to the sinner a perfect righteousness (or "rightness with God") wholly acceptable to God Himself, for He is the One who has provided it. It is called the righteousness of God because it is in contrast to the righteousness man has been trying to achieve for himself. But God is willing to reckon His righteousness to the penitent sinner solely on the gound of his faith in Jesus, and not on the ground of his works; He "righteousifies" him by faith. This is the great message of the epistle to the Romans and this is the basic blessing of the gospel, referred to as justification by faith.

It is important, however, to make clear that though these truths have their first application to a man's initial salvation, they also have a lot for the man who has already become a Christian, but has fallen into sin. It is not suggested that the justified sinner is in and out of justification according to the standard of his walk. If that were so, it would put him back under law and he would not know where he stood. Our justification is eternal and invariable and altogether of grace. But whereas a Christian does not lose his salvation when sin comes in, he does lose fellowship with the One who has saved him – until he confesses his sin. Till then he certainly does lose the joys he has been walking in (a serious loss indeed), but all is restored when he repents, and the very truths by which he first entered are the very truths by which he returns.

Justification is therefore not a dry doctrine, but a living up-to-date thing, very much a *now* experience. "Being justified *now* by His blood …"[6]

Justifying the ungodly

We can easily conceive of God justifying the righteous, for He Himself commanded the Old Testament judges, that "they shall justify the righteous and condemn the wicked."[7] But in the epistle to the Romans we are called to something quite different, even revolutionary. We are called upon to "believe on Him that justifies the ungodly" – the very opposite of what we would expect. It hardly seems moral for Him to justify the ungodly, especially in view of what He has already said to earthly judges. But if it is true, it certainly gives us sinners a chance, for we all struggle with an innate ungodliness. But for a man with a sensitive conscience it certainly takes some believing that God should justify the self-confessed ungodly one.

Romans chapter four assumes that it will pose a

---

[6]Romans 5:9   [7]Deuteronomy 25:1.

problem of faith for some because it goes on to quote Abraham's struggle with unbelief when he was called upon to believe the promised impossibility that he and Sarah would have a child when they were completely beyond age. It is sometimes as hard to believe that God justifies me, the ungodly one, as it was for Abraham to believe that he and Sarah would have a child at their age. He was called to believe for a physical impossibility; you and I for a moral impossibility.[8] But if we will believe in a God of grace and, like Abraham, "against hope believe in hope" and "not stagger at the promise of God through unbelief", but be fully persuaded that God's promise is to be taken as an accomplished fact, that faith of ours will be counted to us for a righteousness to which we are otherwise complete strangers.

We are not saying that He *imparts* righteousness to the sinner, but that He *imputes* it (all the difference in the world); because of this righteousness he may know himself acceptable to God, sinner though he be. Being justified by faith is not the same as being made righteous in *practice* (like Jesus the righteous One). God declares or accounts me righteous even in rags! It was while the prodigal was still in rags that the father said, "Bring forth the best robe and put it on him."[9] The knowledge of this grace is very affecting to the one on the receiving end and puts him under a motivation to holiness such as nothing else will. But none of the new desires and

---

[8]Romans 4:21–25.   [9]Luke 15:22.

constraints that the Spirit works within us are the ground of our new relationship with God – only the blood of Jesus. "Being now justified by His blood"[1].

Not even the archangel Gabriel has a better righteousness before God than I have. Indeed, I am told, "Christ Himself is made to me righteousness."[2] That was the final, liberating truth for John Bunyan. Still lacking assurance, and fearful lest he had committed the unforgivable sin, he was pacing his garden when there came a voice from heaven, "Thy righteousness is in heaven!" He searched his Bible to find where such a verse might be, and he found it, "Christ Jesus, who of God is made unto us … righteousness."[2] From that moment John Bunyan was, as we say, "clean over Jordan".

> Behold Him there, the risen Lamb!
>   My perfect, spotless righteousness,
> The great unchangeable I AM,
>   The King of glory and of grace.

All this on the basis of the cross

Paul, having stated "that we are justified by His grace as a gift", is careful to adds the words, "through the redemption that is in Christ Jesus, whom God has set forth to be a propitiation through faith in His blood."[3] It is only on the basis of the blood of Jesus that we are justified.

But, you say, why the blood, why bring that in

---

[1]Romans 5:9.   [2]1 Corinthians 1:30.   [3]Romans 3:25.

here? Paul answers that question in his next sentence – "to declare His righteousness." We are used to the concept that the sacrifice of Jesus on the cross was *to declare God's love.* Here we are also told it was *to declare God's righteousness.* Justice had to be done with regard to our sins, and seen to be done. And it was done. Jesus died, the Just for the unjust, to bring us to God. It was not only loving of God to put away our sins by the sacrifice of His Son, but just of Him to do it that way. Romans 5:18 says, "By one act of righteousness the free gift came unto all men to justification of life."[4] Calvary was not only an act of love, but an act of righteousness. The due reward of our sins has been exacted at the hands of Another.

Paul goes on to show that the work of the cross avails retrospectively as well as for the present. When Abraham believed on the Lord and it was counted to him for righteousness, his faith did not have his sins in mind, but rather the son that was promised. Yet that faith was counted to him for righteousness. What about his sins? Were they forgiven? The answer is Yes and No. He had righteousness imputed to him, but his sins were not forgiven then; they were only "passed over in the forbearance of God",[5] to use the expression in Romans chapter three. They had yet to be laid on the Lamb of God and their dread price paid by His blood. God passed them over in anticipation of that great day of settling. So when Jesus hung paying the

[4]Romans 5:18. [5]Romans 3:25.

price in His own body on the tree, it was God declaring His righteousness in passing over the sins of the Old Testament saints. One arm of the cross of Jesus went back to the dawn of history to settle the account of the Old Testament debt, and the other arm to the end of history to settle in anticipation the sins committed since the cross. The cross declares it was righteous and just of God to pass over the sins of Old Testament penitents, as it is just of Him now to justify those who believe in Jesus.[6]

All apart from works

Inasmuch as this is a matter of grace, Paul says, "We conclude that a man is justified by faith apart from the works of the law."[7] Note the words, "apart from", which means "without any reference to", whether the works be good or bad. Your good is not going to help you, and your bad, if duly confessed, need be no hindrance. Do all the good you can by all means, but understand it is not going to help your standing with God by one iota. Righteousness is going to be reckoned to you as a matter of gift from first to last and therefore it will be securely yours right to the end.

God has put His ban on the way of works for more reasons than one. The way of works often is really an attempt to put God in our debt. That is clearly taught in the passage we have before us, "Now to him that worketh is the reward not reck-

[6]Romans 3:26.   [7]Romans 3:28.

oned of grace but of debt."[8] If a man gets a reward by his works, the reward has been earned and certainly is not grace! God says, "Who hath first given to Me that I should recompense him again?"[9] The answer is, "No one." We shall get nothing from Him as a matter of debt, only as a gift of charity – it is that or nothing.

Paul and James

One cannot leave this aspect of faith-apart-from-works without conceding the fact that the apostle James seems at first to strike a contradictory note, especially when he says in his epistle, "Ye see then how that by works a man is justified, and not by faith only."[1] What makes it even more strange is that the two Old Testament characters whom James quotes to illustrate what he is saying[2] are the same two that Paul quotes in his epistles to illustrate what he is saying, Abraham[3] in the Romans epistle and Rahab[4] in that to the Hebrews (that is, assuming that the Hebrews epistle was written by Paul).

If we look carefully at the two pairs of verses we shall find that they are not really contradictory, but complementary. Paul emphasises the great truth that God justifies men by faith alone, while James emphasises that faith needs to be justified, or demonstrated as genuine, by what a man is impelled to do because of it. A different corrobo-

---

[8]Romans 4:4   [9]Romans 11:35.   [1]James 2:24.
[2]James 2:21, 25.   [3]Romans 4:1–3.   [4]Hebrews 11:31.

rating action is quoted in each case by which their prior faith was shown to be true, or if you prefer it, justified.

I will not add more, but leave the reader to look up the verses concerned and sort it all out himself. I do not want to do his homework for him. But I would say this much, that every commitment of faith needs to be clinched and demonstrated as real by the stands we take, the decisions we make and the actions we are impelled to, as a result of it. Look carefully and you will see that both Abraham and Rahab are quoted as taking certain actions which they would never have taken had their faith not been genuine, and thus by those works was it justified. Here then is a riddle or puzzle for you to work on – what were the corroborating actions that these two characters took, by which their faith was justified?

Not apart from repentance

Even as we say that justification is apart from works, we have to insist that it is not apart from repentance. Even if we stress it is by faith, we have even than to make it clear that saving faith nearly always implies repentance.

Take, for instance, the verse we have been quoting, "To him that worketh not, but believeth on Him that justifieth the ungodly"; that implies taking the sinner's place, does it not? How can we believe on Him who justifies the ungodly without confessing that we are ungodly ourselves, ungodly in our reactions if not in our actions, even though we profess to be Christians.

Another reason for God's ban on the way of works is that it can sometimes be a polite substitute for repentance, in spite of the fact that the Word says "to obey is better than sacrifice and to hearken than the fat of rams."[5] Such are our deceitful hearts that we would far rather climb up into the sheepfold some other way, even at great cost to ourselves, than bend our necks to enter the low door of repentance.

Holiness will follow, motivated by love, for "he that is forgiven much loveth much."[6] The release of spirit that comes through repentance and "seeing the blood" again is so great that the emancipated one will do anything for the Beloved who has done it all for him, not in order to be blessed, which would be works, but because he has been blessed, which is grace. In this way "faith worketh by love",[7] and when faith works, it really works. Works do not, therefore, precede justification, but follow it as a happy and natural consequence. Holiness comes in by the back door, as the consequence, not the cause. Oh, the delightful stratagem of grace!

> *I cannot work my soul to save,*
> *For that my Lord hath done;*
> *But I would work like any slave*
> *For love of God's dear Son.*

---

[5] 1 Samuel 15:22. [6] Luke 7:47. [7] Galatians 5:6.

Believing on God who declares him to be right who confesses himself to be wrong

This is the point to which we have come. We are to believe on a God who declares him to be right who confesses himself to be wrong – therefore be quick to admit you are wrong. The grace that meets us when we do so is the biggest incentive of all for us to take the sinner's place. In an argument or a discussion when everybody is pressing their point of view and insisting they are right, how refreshing it is when someone admits he is wrong. A fresh wind begins to blow, at least as far as that one man is concerned. But how hard it is to find a sinner! Little wonder that God so often finds His hands tied.

Take the parable of the publican and pharisee.[8] The publican, unlike the pharisee, stood afar off at the back of the temple and smote upon his breast saying, "God be merciful to me, a sinner." Perhaps up till then he had blamed other people, his wife, his kids, his colleagues, for his bad spirit. But that day God triumphed over him when he said, in effect, "I am the one who is wrong – wrong with You, O God, and with everybody else." What was the response of Deity to that brokenness? Jesus said, "I tell you, this man went down to his house justified rather than the other." Perhaps God had had to wait a long time to hear him say, "I am the sinner." But the Holy Spirit had won the victory in him and Jesus declared him to be right who

---

[8]Luke 18:13, 14.

confessed he was wrong – right above all with God.

We, too, having confessed that we are wrong, have to believe God's word that we are now right with Him. Sometimes it is as hard to believe we are right, in view of all our failures, as to confess we are wrong – but He helps us to get through to faith.

I often have two battles. The first is to admit I am wrong. I find it hard because I am a proud man and I hate to admit that I am wrong, whether to God or to others. Having at last done it, I have a second battle – to believe I am right, right with God by the blood of Jesus. That battle with an accusing conscience can be as severe as any battle with a stubborn will. But I have to win that battle, I have to believe in the power of the blood; against hope I have got to believe in hope, as Abraham did, and I have to believe on "Him that justifieth the ungodly". Above all I must "believe on Him that raised up Jesus our Lord from the dead"[9] as a sign that the blood of His Son was sufficient for Him and therefore it is sufficient for me. Then peace comes again, and I stand afresh on redemption ground. I have had a similar battle with unbelief as Abraham had, but have become "fully persuaded that what God has promised He is able also to perform" and righteousness is imputed to me as it was to Abraham.[1]

With this new experience of justification by faith, it does not matter what others think of me. It is God, the highest of all, who justifies me, though I turn to

---

[9]Romans 4:24, 25.   [1]Romans 4:23, 24.

Him in rags. If any should come and share their misgivings about me, I can agree with them and say, "You are right. God has shown me the same, but He has cleansed me in the blood of Jesus and justified me." If God, then, be for us when we admit we are wrong, who then can be against us?

"A certain man had two sons; and he came to the first, and said, Son, go work today in my vineyard. He answered and said, I will not: but afterward, he repented, and went. And he came to the second, and said likewise. And he answered and said, I go, Sir: and went not. Whether of the two did the will of his father? They say unto Him, The first. Jesus saith unto them, Verily, I say unto you, That the publicans and the harlots go into the kingdom of God before you" (Matthew 21:28–31).

"But now God commandeth all men everywhere to repent, because He hath appointed a day in which He will judge the world in righteousness, by that Man whom He hath ordained" (Acts 17:30–31).

"Be zealous, therefore, and repent" (Revelation 3:19).

9

REPENTANCE
for sinner and saint

The primacy of the call to repentance can hardly be overrated. Whether God's call is directed to a lost world, or to a redeemed but needy church, His first word is "repent". Jesus Himself began His teaching; "Repent, for the Kingdom of Heaven is at hand."[1]

These were also the first words that His forerunner, John the Baptist, uttered, "Repent ye, for the Kingdom of Heaven is at hand."[2]

It was Peter's answer to the people on the Day of Pentecost when they realised that the One whom they had crucified was their Messiah, now risen from the dead. They cried out in conviction of sin, "Men and brethren, what shall we do? Peter said unto them, Repent."[3]

Repentance is the key by which all the blessings of the Gospel are opened to us.

It is a mistake to think that this is only a word for the lost; it is also for the Christian. In the early chapters of the book of Revelation the risen Lord sent His message through the apostle John to the seven

---

[1]Matthew 4:17.   [2]Matthew 3:2.   [3]Acts 2:38.

churches of that day. To five out of the seven of the churches His message was, "Repent".[4]

He told those churches that though there was much about them of which He approved, He had something against them and His call to them was not to try harder, or make promises, or be more devout, but to repent. One church was bidden to "repent and do the first works." They had left their first love. To another of the churches the message was, "Be zealous therefore and repent." We all feel it is proper for Christians to be zealous; zealous in prayer, zealous in witnessing to others, in winning souls, in church work. Jesus would say to us, in all your zeal first be zealous in repenting.

What is repentance?

What do we actually understand by the word, *repent?* The Greek word translated in our Bibles "repent" means to change your mind. Jesus told a parable about two sons who were both sent to work in their father's vineyard. One of them stiffened his neck and said, "'I will not,' *but afterward he repented and went.*"[5] In other words, he changed his mind.

But many preachers and Bible teachers have added extra facets in an attempt to strengthen its content. Yes, they say, it means to change your mind. but also to change your direction, and change your behaviour, and change your outlook and live a new

---

[4]Revelation 2:5, 16, 22 and Revelation 3:3, 19.
[5]Matthew 21:29.

life. This is done in the laudable attempt to save the Christian message from appearing to connive at a "sinning and repenting syndrome." The trouble with that presentation is that there is so much doing to be done on our part that it ends up with being inconsistent with grace.

The experience of Martin Luther is a case in point. I believe I am right in saying that the Roman Catholic Bible of his day translated the word, repent, as, "do penance", so that well-known texts came out as "Do penance, for the Kingdom of Heaven is at hand", "Do penance and believe the gospel". Martin Luther took this seriously and tried to do penance, but he never knew whether he had done enough, and therefore was never sure if he were saved.

It was only when he learnt that the Greek word was to change your mind, that the light broke in upon him and he saw that salvation is by grace through faith, and that a change of mind which agreed with God and took the sinner's place was the only necessary preliminary for exercising saving faith in Jesus. Whether modern Roman Catholic Bibles use the word penance, I do not know, but German evangelical Christians to this day are still saddled with that word. When I am preaching by interpretation and use the word "repent", they often translate it "Busse tun". But they, of course, do not read into it the same meaning that poor Martin Luther did. There is another word for repent ("bereuen") they could use, and I wish that they would.

"Right in our own eyes"

To repent, then, simply means to change one's mind and can be used with regard to changing our minds about anything. But when the word is used about man's relationship with God it means changing our mind about one thing – our righteousness.

Man, whether he is religious or utterly irreligious, is a moral being. He can never get away from it; issues of right and wrong are deeply embedded in his being. The actual standards of right and wrong may vary somewhat from person to person, but everybody has standards of some sort, and certainly he has them for the other person! A man resents nothing more than being accused of being wrong when he thinks he is correct. Why does he not readily say, "If I am wrong, I don't care. It doesn't matter to me." But he cannot and will not take such an attitude, unless he is in the very last stages of moral deterioration. He has to justify himself and work out some sort of moral alibi for himself, or at least plead extenuating circumstances. The most depraved prostitute could not live with herself unless she could produce some such rationalisation or excuse, if only to say that hers is the oldest profession in the world.

The reason for this is found in the Book of Proverbs, "Every way of a man is right in his own eyes."[6] That is man's basic attitude and that is where

---

[6]Proverbs 21:2.

God has to begin with him. God's Word tells a man that he is a sinner and specifies matters where he is at fault. But that is something he will not have: he is right in his own eyes. Therefore he "rejects the counsel of God against himself",[7] exactly as the Pharisees did. Immediately, in effect, he makes God a liar ("if we say we have not sinned we make Him a liar and His Word is not in us")[8]. His relationship with God is now one of enmity because he is unwilling to acknowledge he is the sinner God says he is. The reaction of self-justification is automatic. At the mere suggestion he is wrong, he will insist he is right, either before God or his fellows.

That is where he must repent; that is the point where God presses him hard to change his mind. God will wrestle with him, as the angel wrestled with Jacob, sometimes till the breaking of the day, until he says in deep sincerity, "Oh God, You are right and I am wrong." This is absolutely crucial. We call it being broken. It is not a matter of tears and emotions, but of the will; we become willing to take the sinner's place and say we are wrong. We relinquish our own righteousness and take the sinner's place. When Jesus took the same place, which was mine, "He was made of no reputation". It should not surprise me if my reputation goes too.

But if in repenting I lose my reputation, I gain Christ in a new way. Paul found himself the gainer and you will, too. Paul said, "I count all things but

---

[7]Luke 7:30.   [8]1 John 1:10.

loss for the excellency of the knowledge of Christ
Jesus my Lord."[9] Excellency is that which excels,
and what he found in Jesus utterly excelled what he
lost of his own righteousness.

In this way, David's word in his psalm of confession is fulfilled, "that Thou mightest be justified
when Thou speakest, and be clear when Thou
judgest." If nothing else is proved by David's sin
and ours, it is that God is right in all that He has said
about us, and by our repentance and confession we
justify Him. "Thou has done right, but we have
done wickedly",[1] prayed the Levites of old.

If my people shall humble themselves

Repentance can be very humbling and that is why
the Old Testament often uses for the sinner's
response to Deity the phrase "humble thyself".
Whereas "repent" is the New Testament word,
"humble thyself" is the more usual phrase in the
Old Testament. If true repentance means a man
saying, "Oh God, you are right and I am wrong," it
is a humbling experience.

It is a moving study to go through the thirty
occurrences of the phrase (you can perhaps look
them up in the marginal references in your Bible).
Here are a few of them to give you the flavour of
their deep message.

"Seest thou how Ahab humbleth himself before
Me?"[2]

---

[9]Philippians 3:8.   [1]Nehemiah 9:33.   [2]1 Kings 21:29.

"Because thy heart was tender and thou has humbled thyself before the Lord, when thou heardest what I spake against this place and against the inhabitants thereof … and thou hast rent thy clothes and wept before Me; I also have heard thee, saith the Lord."[3]

"Notwithstanding Hezekiah humbled himself for the pride of his heart."[4]

"And when Mannasseh was in affliction, he besought the Lord his God and humbled himself greatly before the God of his fathers."[5]

"And Zedekiah humbled not himself before Jeremiah the prophet speaking from the mouth of the Lord."[6]

In five places the New Testament uses the phrase to express the same thought and does so to great effect. For example, "He that humbleth himself shall be exalted",[7] and "Humble yourself therefore under the mighty hand of God that He may exalt you in due time" etc.[8] Above all in the New Testament, this phrase is applied to Jesus Himself: "and being found in fashion as a man, He humbled Himself, becoming obedient unto death, even the death of the cross."[9] In taking the sinner's place on the cross, when He was not a sinner, Jesus the sinless One surely humbled Himself.

---

[3]2 Kings 22:19.   [4]2 Chronicles 32:26.   [5]2 Chronicles 33:12.
[6]2 Chronicles 36:12.   [7]Matthew 23:12.   [8]1 Peter 5:6.
[9]Philippians 2:8.

Family tree of repentance

Repentance is, as we have explained, a changed attitude. But an attitude has to be expressed, in word and deed. We could say that repentance has two sons. First, confession of sin, which is repentance in word. Once you are willing to change your mind and admit you are wrong, you have to confess it as sin to God, and verbalise your repentance in words. You say, "Do I really have to do that? He knows it already, surely." His answer to that is clear: "Take with you words and turn to the Lord."[1] I do not know why, but He asks you to do it. Perhaps He knows it will do something to you to hear yourself confessing your sins in words. If that be the case, don't think your prayer, speak it, even when you are on your own! I often do. Also it will be sometimes obvious to us that an apology is owing to another. Beware, however, lest you get into bondage to self-made rules about how much you should share. God will show.

The other son is restitution, which is repentance in deed. I once saw a question down as the subject of a talk, "Can a sinner be forgiven and yet retain the offence?" The answer clearly is, no. Zacchaeus was forgiven his misdeeds as a corrupt tax collector. He received Jesus into his home and in the gladness of his heart made restitution to those whom he had defrauded. Indeed, for good measure, he restored four times as much as he had unlawfully taken. That

---

[1] Hosea 14:2.

was repenting in style, and was certainly the sort of salvation that his clients did not object to! Here, too, you will need God's guidance and the counsel of wise Christian friends to resolve some tricky problems of restitution.

But be clear about this, these are only the children of repentance, and not repentance itself. You cannot confess what you have not clearly repented of and the same is true of making restitution. First, get it clear that you have repented before God, that you are the wrong one and that you plead no extenuating circumstances, that you are no longer "right in your own eyes"; and, more than that, that you have already appropriated your forgiveness through grace and the blood of Christ. Then confession and, if necessary, restitution follow, the sons, the consequences of repentance.

Negative and the positive

Here is something that I have found most helpful: entering into the positive by repenting of the negative. If we are aware of the lack of some special quality in our Christian lives, the obvious thing would be for us to ask God to supply it according to the Scripture, "If any man lack wisdom (or anything else) let him ask of God that giveth to all men liberally".[2] I do not always find that gets me very far. If I am asking God for something, that implies that I have not got it. Then why not begin

---

[2] James 1:5.

by confessing that fact to God? I am finding that the major part of asking is confessing that I have not got it (whatever it may be) and doing so deeply and restfully. In this way I am presenting to God my emptiness, which is exactly what He wants; for confessed emptiness is ever the way to fulness. In this way I become a candidate for grace, if only by my very lacks. In other words, I enter into the positive by confessing the negative. This is what I have already called entering by the back door, the beggar's door. Grace gives me a welcome every time I come as a beggar and delights to give what I confess I have not got!

If you lack love for a difficult person, do not just ask for love, but repent of unlove (better, call it hate) and you are not only forgiven hate, but given love, divine love. God delights to put into you what He wants out of you, but which you confess isn't there. If you lack courage, do not in the first place ask for courage, but rather go deeper, repent of fear, and with God's forgiveness of the sin of fear, you will be given courage, His courage. If you lack peace of heart, do not plead for peace, but repent of worry and unbelief and see the sinfulness of them, and with forgiveness there is given peace. If you lack the fulness of the Holy Spirit, confess that lack to Him; tell Him frankly, as I have often done; "Lord, one thing is certain to me at this moment of time, I am not filled with the Spirit, and yet in a moment or two I have to preach." Don't ask for fulness, confess emptiness; and as sure as grace is grace you will be filled and anointed.

I say again, confessed emptiness is the way to fulness. The Holy Spirit is not the reward of your faithfulness, but God's gift for your weakness, and surely you have plenty of that. In this way we enter into the positive blessing we need by confessing the negative, which means we enter by the blood of Jesus. For it is by faith in that blood alone that we have boldness and a new approach to a God of grace.

Primacy of repentance

In closing this chapter I return to the primacy of repentance. If the saints never repent, or are never heard to do so, neither will the lost repent. The time has come when judgment, that is self-judgment, must begin at the house of God. If it begins with us, where shall the ungodly and the sinner appear? Where, indeed? When they hear and see it, first they will be astonished, then they will be shorn of every excuse; and finally, they will join the brethren, hopefully, at the foot of the cross of Jesus, repenting also. Notice in that verse in Peter's epistle, it is all contingent on, "if it begin at us".[3]

I heard a dear brother say once, "Where there is no revival everybody is right. When revival comes, that is, when Jesus Himself comes, everybody is wrong" – even those considered the best. One can judge the degree of the presence of God in the midst, by the degree of conviction of sin and the response of repentance manifested.

---

[3] 1 Peter 4:17.

In Uganda, during the times of revival that God has been giving them for so long, a certain chief was gloriously saved. He was one of the Africans whom the British authorities (Uganda was still a British Protectorate) were grooming for government service. He was sent to England to attend a special course of study and it was during that time he came to the Holiday Conference at Abergele, North Wales, in which I was involved. He was an impressive, well-built man, middle-aged, with hair beginning to grey – and a new Christian full of the joy of the Lord. One of our team of speakers, on learning that he had already spent some weeks in London, asked him if he had heard Dr Martyn Lloyd-Jones preach – at that time at the height of his powers and beloved by many on both sides of the Atlantic.

"No," he replied, "I have not heard him."

"Oh, you should try and do that," said my friend. "He is one of our greatest English preachers." He went on to describe his excellencies.

The African chief listened patiently. Eventually, when my friend had run out of breath, he just asked one question.

"Does he repent?"

To him there were but two sorts of Christians, casual Christians and those who repented and he had just become one of the latter! I knew personally and appreciated Dr Lloyd-Jones and knew how much on stretch for revival he was. But what a question to ask of anybody, eminent preacher, or man in the pew! "Does he repent?" It tells it all and flattens every distinction. It is the one thing that God is concerned about for each of us, and it is the one thing well within our reach. "Does he repent?" Start with the first thing you know is sin. If it is true that you are a man who does not repent, confess that fact to God; let that be the first big negative with which you come to Him. And you have begun! You have entered into the new relationship and walk with the Lord and you only need now to go on with the same steps with which you have begun, as occasion demands.

In a book on John Wesley I found a beautiful summary of the message he preached and which was at the heart of the eighteenth century revival when great companies of people all over the land were gathered into the Kingdom of God. *"His constant theme was salvation by faith apart from works preceded by repentance and followed by holiness"*.

To that could be added Oswald Chambers' word about "conscious repentance leading to unconscious holiness". I am not sure I like the idea of a "conscious holiness," but an "unconscious holiness" – that is very different! "Conscious repentance" leads there every time.

Ideally the Christian life should begin with repentance and then go on in faith, but in practice often we begin in faith and go on, if we go on at all, in repentance. Yet it is the way to go on with Jesus. A dear friend of mine, now in heaven, used to end her letters to me, "Yours repenting and rejoicing."

"Therefore being justified by faith, we have peace with God through our Lord Jesus Christ; by whom also we have access by faith into this grace wherein we stand, and rejoice in hope of the glory of God. And not only so but we glory in tribulations also" (Romans 5:1–3).

" … and whom He called, them He also justified: and whom He justified, them He also glorified" (Romans 8:30).

" … if so be that we suffer with Him, that we may be also glorified together with Him. For I reckon that the sufferings of this present time are not worthy to be compared with the glory that shall be revealed in us" Romans 8:17–18).

"For if we believe that Jesus died and rose again, even so them also which sleep in Jesus will God bring with Him. For this we say unto you by the Word of the Lord, that we which are alive and remain unto the coming of the Lord shall not precede them which are asleep. For the Lord Himself shall descend from heaven with a shout, with the voice of the archangel, and with the trump of God: and the dead in Christ shall rise first: then we which are alive and remain shall be caught up together with them in the clouds, to meet the Lord in the air: and so shall we ever be with the Lord" (1 Thessalonians 4:14–17).

10

GLORIFICATION
for the redeemed

In the New Testament heaven is not always called heaven. In Paul's writings he usually calls it glory, as when he tells us at the beginning of Romans chapter five that now he is justified by faith, he has not only peace with God, but he "rejoices in hope of the glory of God. "[1] Glory seems to be his characteristic word. When one of the believers of the early early days went to be with the Lord, it was said he had been glorified. What a wonderful word! A believer was glorified when he had gone into the enjoyment of what the New Testament calls "glory".

I would define glory by one word – splendour. Everything is full of splendour in that place which Jesus has gone to prepare for us. If glory can be called splendour, then to be glorified means to be splendourised! That is what friends will say when they see you in that day, you've been splendourised.

Glory is a direct result of being justified by faith. It says so in that verse already quoted – "therefore being justified by faith, we have peace with God …

---

[1]Romans 5:2.

and rejoice in the hope of the glory of God." Two things result. First, we have peace with God. We can look God in the face; we can stand before Him without a shred of shame. Who is he that shall lay anything to the charge of God's elect, if it is God that justifies?

The second thing promised is, "we rejoice in hope of the glory of God." The worst sinner who has come to the cross of Jesus and repented of his sins and been declared right with God, not only has peace with God, but is given the positive assurance that he is on his way to glory. Of that he need not have a shadow of a doubt. I know it says "Rejoice in hope of the glory of God" and at first sight that word "hope" seems to have an element of doubt about it. But the Greek word translated "hope" is a strong word and means confident expectation. So we rejoice in confident expectation of the glory of God.

We need to express our joy in this confident assurance, and there are many choruses celebrating the believer's assurance that he is on his way to the glory land. We need to sing about it and think about it, and let the light of glory play upon our faces. Such a bright and sure expectation for the future makes all the difference to our present experience of grace. You may have doubts of getting there but God has none. Indeed, He is so sure that you will make it, that He regards you as already there: "whom He justified, them He also glorified."[2]

---

[2]Romans 8:30.

"Wait a minute", you say, "I haven't actually got there yet. In any case, how do I know that I will endure to the end?"

God is going to see to that; indeed He guarantees it. Because God will persevere in grace, you will persevere in holiness! Your place in glory does not depend on your perseverance, but on the presence there of Jesus, your great high Priest and His blood – all for you. As an old hymn says:

> *I know that while in Heaven He stands,*
> *No tongue can bid me thence depart.*

I think I know why Paul felt the people he was writing to needed to be assured. I rather imagine there must have been some, who, when they heard that the wrath of God had been revealed from heaven against all unrighteousness and ungodliness of men,[3] and learnt there was a great day of reckoning coming for the whole world, and that the great white throne would be set up, when the dead, small and great, would stand before God, and the books of every man's life would be opened,[4] and the dead would be judged out of the books according to their works, I believe some of them trembled. They began to wonder where they were. How would it be with them in that great day of reckoning?

So Paul wrote to them in this chapter, "God commendeth his love toward you in that, while you were still sinners, Christ died for you."[5] If, therefore,

---

[3]Romans 1:18.   [4]Revelation 20:12.   [5]Romans 5:8.

they were loved when they were still away from Him, much more, being now justified by His blood, they would be saved from wrath through Him.[6] Dear sinner, who has fled to the cross, and dared to believe the great edict that by the blood of Jesus you have been justified – that day is not for you. You are not going to be there. The world, yes, but not this wonderful company of resurrected ones, whom God has foreknown, called and justified; they are rather going to be glorified.

Glory, however, is not merely negative, and does not only consist in the fact that you are not condemned for your sins.

The greatest thing about glory is that we shall see Jesus face to face. Says Peter, "Whom not having seen, we love."[7] All your pilgrim way you have loved Him, but you have never seen Him – at least, not face to face. There have been many spiritual revelations of Him, but one day in glory we shall see this dear One, face to face.

No more dimly

This verse from Paul's first letter to the Corinthians is appropriate here: "For now we see in a mirror dimly, but then, face to face; now I know only in part, but then shall I know even as also I am known."[8] Every motorist knows the difference between seeing in a mirror and seeing face to face. How glad we are for our driving mirrors; we could

---

[6]Romans 5:9.   [7]1 Peter 1:8.   [8]1 Corinthians 13:12.

not do without them. They are fairly good and one can get an idea of what is behind. But it is much clearer when we see something face to face, as when a car is coming towards us. Some mirrors are cheap and can give a distorted view. But there are others, good ones, which give a correct view.

According to this verse we see Jesus now in a mirror, not face to face. Praise God for the mirror in which we see Jesus – the Word of God by the Spirit's anointing, as we read it and hear it preached. But the mirror is also somewhat associated with our own understanding. Some people, as they share Jesus, give us a wider perspective of Him. Others a narrower – a more detailed one. That is how it should be. It needs different mirrors to increase our understanding of the Lord Jesus Christ and the way of grace. Of course, our mirror can be distorted. The Bible is not distorted, but our understanding of it may be and for a number of reasons.

But the day is coming when we are not going to see Him in a mirror any more; we are going to see Him face to face. That is going to be the pre-eminent experience of glory.

There was a young woman who had had many sad experiences. She lost her husband, then her child, and then later, she herself lay dying. She loved the Lord and was a true believer, and someone who was attending her said, "It won't be long now, dear, and you will see Harry and the little baby boy."

Do you know what she said?

"Jesus first!"

I believe we can be a bit sentimental about

meeting others in glory. We say to ourselves, I am going to meet all my loved ones again, what a reunion that will be! But Jesus first!

The Scripture does not make a lot of the reunion of believers with believers; it is implied, but Jesus first!

Will you be looking around glory to see that husband of yours first of all? That is not very honouring to the One who brought you to glory at such great cost! My dear friend, I believe in that day other things will fall away. It will be Jesus first you will want to see. So will your husband. He will be more concerned to see Jesus than even to see you. There will certainly be a reunion, but let us not make too much of that, because it is not the emphasis we get in Scripture.

Look at this verse: "Now I know in part, then shall I know as also I am known."[9] All along Jesus has known me in my sin, and that fully. I have known Him in His grace, but only partly, not fully. But in that day I shall know Him in His grace, as fully as He has known me in my sin. He has known me in my sin and so often had mercy on me. I only feebly have been tasting that grace, but one day I will really know it, even as all along He has known this poor old sinner, and I shall experience a fulness of love and grace beyond anything I have known before.

---

[9] 1 Corinthians 13:12.

Transformed bodies

In glory we are going to experience a glorious resurrection from the dead and be given transformed bodies. Heaven is not going to be peopled with disembodied spirits or ghosts. We are going to have beautiful bodies. "For our citizenship is in heaven; from whence also we look for the Saviour, the Lord Jesus Christ; who shall change the body of our humiliation that it may be like unto the body of His glory, according to the working whereby He is able even to subdue all things unto Himself."[1] These are the days of our humiliation, and these the bodies of our humiliation. It is humiliating not to be able to get out of that chair without assistance because of rheumatism, and to have to depend on other people for so much. But when He comes, He is going to change the body of our humiliation, and it is going to be as good as the body of His glory which He put on at His resurrection.

Do not reject this as being too literal; be grateful you are going to have a new body. It is not going to be the same sort of body; we are definitely told "there is a natural body and a spiritual body"[2] and yours is going to be a spiritual body, but a real body nonetheless. Jesus had a body when He rose. He said, "Handle Me and see, a spirit hath not flesh and bones as you see Me have."[3] But all traces of age and sickness and worry will have gone and I want to assure you, dear reader, you will be better looking

---

[1]Philippians 3:20, 21   [2]1 Corinthians 15:44.   [3]Luke 24:39.

then than you have ever been before! The saints of God will be a fine-looking crowd, possessed of eternal life, with resurrection bodies that shall never know sorrow, disease, or death! I do not know why God is not content for us to be spirits in heaven, but apparently He said, "No, I am going to give you a bonus; you are going to have a lovely body."

Every compensation

In glory we shall be more than compensated for every tear, sorrow, ache, pain, and every injustice done to us. There is a wonderful verse in the epistle to the Romans; "I reckon that the sufferings of this present time are not worthy to be compared with the glory that shall be revealed in us."[4] And again, "If we suffer, we shall also reign with Him."[5]

Paul was in a bad state sometimes; he was not a fit man; he had to spend a night and a day in the deep on one occasion, and that didn't help his rheumatism. He spent more time in Roman prisons than anybody would want, but he went on muttering that he reckoned that the sufferings of this present time were not worthy to be compared with the glory that was to be revealed for him. He had his eye on glory all the time and he had the light of it on his face.

There are going to be marvellous compensations for you, even in anticipation; and in glory itself you will have no cause to complain.

---

[4]Romans 8:18.   [5]2 Timothy 2:12.

Manifestation of God's aristocracy

Paul continues the verse that speaks about the glory that shall be revealed in us with the words, "For the earnest expectation of creation waiteth for the manifestation of the sons of God."[6] It goes on to tell us that this world has been made subject to vanity. A strange expression, but it simply means that weeds now grow much more readily than the fruit we want. We are cursed with droughts and famines. This earth has been affected by the fall of man in all sorts of different ways – but it is waiting for its emancipation from the bondage of corruption to be a new earth; something which is going to happen when the sons of God are manifested. Those sons of God may not seem very important now, but they are God's aristocracy, and will be shown to be such, when the great day of their manifestation comes. When that happens "the creation itself shall also be delivered from the bondage of corruption into the glorious liberty of the children of God."[7] It is all there in Romans chapter 8. Read it.

That will be a great parade when the saints are manifested to a wondering creation as God's nobility.

Then shall be fulfilled that which was spoken of by the apostle John, "Behold, what manner of love the father hath bestowed upon us that we should be called the sons of God."[8] You may well marvel at the love that has made you manifest as God's son, when

---

[6]Romans 8:19.   [7]Romans 8:21.   [8]1 John 3:1.

you recall that you once said in the words of the prodigal, "I am not worthy to be called thy son." All the more wonder that He has acknowledged you now to be one of His aristocracy!

The verse just quoted goes on, "therefore the world knoweth us not because they knew Him not."[9] They knew neither Him nor us. They do not know who is amongst them. They do not know that that humble Christian is one day going to shine like a star in heaven. "But we know that when He shall appear we shall be like Him; for we shall see Him as He is."[1] There is going to be a great and glorious parade when the saints go marching in, and they are going to rule with Christ over His creation for ever and ever.

When will this glory be?

When shall we enter this glory? The quick answer is not until the trumpet sounds and the Lord Jesus comes the second time. This is the hope of the ages.

You may be disappointed to hear that; you had always thought, "I go to heaven when I die", and you ask, "Is that not so?" The answer I would give is Yes and No. It is true that Paul says he has a "desire to depart and be with Christ, which is far better"[2] and in another place he speaks about being "absent from the body and present with the Lord."[3] But the Lord has not come again and this means that we have not been raised from the dead yet, nor

---

[9]1 John 3:1. [1]1 John 3:2. [2]Philippians 1:23. [3]2 Corinthians 5:8.

given our transformed bodies. Nor will we be seeing Jesus as yet face to face, because John's epistle clearly links that with "when He shall appear".[4]

It would seem that we need to wait for that. Some might well say, and I feel like saying it myself, "Well, I don't want to wait." The Thessalonian Christians were a little disappointed when they heard they would have to wait, disappointed because for them in those days the coming of the Lord was imminent, and they felt they would not have to wait long. But they are still waiting!

I have puzzled over this for quite a time – this first instalment of going to be with the Lord and then the long wait for the major part, the final instalment of glory. I have wondered if perhaps the use of the expression "them that sleep in Jesus" might provide a clue. It could be said that when you fall into a deep sleep the next thing you are conscious of is waking to a new morning the next day, unconscious of the passage of time. Even so, we might awake in the same way on the resurrection morning, unconscious there had been any waiting.

I was not sure that satisfied me. Only recently, bit by bit, has the Lord given me an answer which is both satisfying and utterly thrilling. I shared this puzzle with my wife and said, "Frankly, I don't know what to think." Then it was the Lord began to show me what I felt I needed to see and used, amongst other things, a quotation from Martin

---

[4]1 John 3:2.

Luther. It was another case of entering into the positive by confessing the negative, of coming to know by confessing ignorance.

Before time began

The thing that characterises life on earth is time. Time is specially associated with this universe, in that we measure it by the sun and moon. Time had a beginning, it would seem, because twice in Paul's epistles he has the phrase, "Before time began".[5] The Authorised Version has it as "before the world began", but the word "world" there is different from the usual one. The usual word for world is the Greek *kosmos* and is found in at least 187 places. But there is also *aion*, (used only 32 times) meaning *the age*, or *the ages*, but still the A.V. has it as "world." It seems clear to me that it is right to adopt the readings of the New International Version, "before the beginning of time"; the New King James Version, "before time began"; or the old Revised Version, "before times eternal".

It is right, then, to conceive of a moment before God set His great clock of time ticking. Will that clock ever cease? I think so. Revelation 10:6 in the A.V. tells of the prophetic angel that lifted up his hand to heaven and swore by Him that liveth for ever and ever "that there should be time no longer". I know that most newer translations make that phrase "that there should be delay no longer"; and

[5] 2 Timothy 1:9 and Titus 1:2 (Greek *aion*).

that certainly seems to help us with a simple meaning. But the fact is that the Greek word for time is *chronos* and is translated "time" in 30 places and never with any other word associated with delay, although I would not be dogmatic with regard to the interpretation of this verse.

It is difficult for the finite mind to conceive of a state of things before time. But out there before time began, Paul's two verses tell us God did two things: He formed in His own heart a purpose of grace for us sinners, and He made us a promise of eternal life. All that happened before time began; and way before the foundation of the world. The world was founded in time, but these good purposes for sinners were made before time had even begun to tick. God's plan of salvation for sinners was no after-thought! When you talk about grace, you have to go back to that unimaginable past "before time began." One of Beverley Shea's earliest songs contained the lines,

> *Long before time began,*
> *You were part of His plan.*

Time and eternity

The thing that characterises life on earth is time. Beyond earth is eternity. Eternity is not elongated time, but non-time, or what we might call, timeless-ness. All sorts of great things might be happening there which would never take up any of our time. In eternity God has no past, and there is no future.

Everything is present tense. The past history of the world is present, so is also the future – it has already happened; everything in history and what we would call the future – all is present. That is why He can talk about His beloved Son as the Lamb slain from the foundation of the world. The Lamb did die on earth at a definite point in time from our point of view. But with God Calvary was already accomplished out of time.

The contrast between a book and a reader reading it may help us. As the reader comes to a definite point in the story, that point is present tense to him and he is enjoying it at that moment. But it has a past which he has already read and a future which he is yet to read. But he can turn to any other point in the story and that part immediately becomes present tense to him. The book is in time, but the reader, whom we may represent as God, is in eternity. Any, or all of it, can at his will be the present for him. During my lifetime I have been locked into time, but at death I return to God who made me and I pass from time into eternity, and everything is the present to me as it is to Him.

When a child of God dies

When a child of God comes to die he passes out of time into eternity, where all the greatest historical essentials of the faith have already been accomplished; the trumpet has sounded, the Lord has come, men have been raised from their graves, the saints have received their resurrection bodies and

Jesus Himself is seen face to face and reigns in the midst. Of that day Martin Luther said, "Immediately I die, I shall hear a kindly voice say, 'Martin, it is time to get up' and I shall rise." Has he waited a long time, or a short time? It is irrelevant; we have finished with time, we are in eternity, and as far as the saint's consciousness, it is immediate. Sudden death, if such it is to be, is sudden glory!

How marvellous it all is! What a contrast there is between the manner of our dying with the manner of our rising, between the sordidness and sometimes pain of our leaving, with the glory of our entering in. "It is sown in corruption; it is raised in incorruption. It is sown in dishonour; it is raised in glory; it is sown in weakness; it is raised in power. It is sown a natural body; it is raised a spiritual body."[6] Someone has said that death is the final obscenity and from one point of view it would seem so (even the New Testament calls death, "the last enemy"), but the glory that is ahead gilds the bed of death with light.

The real sting of death is not the pain of a terminal illness, the Bible says, but sin. God's Son has removed that sting. A mother called her child frightened by a bee and surrounded her in her arms. After a moment the mother said, "Now you may safely go, dear." The bee had stung the mother's arm and lost its sting there and the child was free. The sting of death is sin, but it has lost its sting in stinging the Lord Jesus on the cross; sin can no longer accuse or

---

[6] 1 Corinthians 15:42–44.

condemn you now. Thus Jesus has "abolished death and brought life and immortality to light through the gospel" and has made even death our servant.

I once heard Dr Martyn Lloyd-Jones preach on Paul's words, "All things are yours … and ye are Christ's and Christ is God's."[7] In that verse the apostle ennumerates the things which he says are "yours", such as Paul, Apollos, or Cephas, or the world, or life or death, or things present, or things to come, all are yours. Dr Lloyd-Jones picked on that word, death. "In what sense", he asked, "can death be said to be ours?" He answered his own question, "In this sense – death is our servant, he is the porter that opens the door and lets us into glory, and as we enter we bow and say thank you to him." True, Scripture calls him the last enemy and yet Jesus has so overcome him that He has turned our enemy into our servant. We need not be afraid of death. He is our servant in that he helps us over that last step into glory. As an old hymn says, Jesus is the "death of death and hell's destruction."

The lost?

What shall we say of the lost, those who have not repented and availed themselves of Jesus and His blood? We call them lost, but they are not lost merely on the last day; they were lost all the way along. That is the biblical word to describe their condition – lost, needing to be found, but all too

---

[7] 1 Corinthians 3:21–23.

often unwilling for that. They, too, pass from time into eternity and everything is in the present tense for them, no need for them to wait until the last judgment. The sins of a lifetime are there in the present, the books are already open as they always have been, the sentence is already sounding out, "Depart from Me, I never knew you." How pathetic if they are going to miss all the joys of glory, which Jesus has bought for them!

C.S. Lewis, in a chapter on hell in his book "The Problem of Pain", has a touching sentence; "So much mercy and yet there is hell!" But the final line has not yet been drawn even if you are still without assurance of His salvation. The door of mercy is open and you can reach it where you are. Be assured, He does not need any persuading to save you. It is you who need persuading – to receive Him and let Him receive you.

Be persuaded today.

RHP One Pound Classics

DAVID WILKERSON
Hungry For More of Jesus
The way of intimacy with Christ
Hallowed Be Thy Names
Knowing God as you've never known Him before

ANDREW MURRAY
The True Vine
Fruitfulness and stability in Jesus

ROY HESSION
The Power of God's Grace
The way of peace, joy and genuine revival
We Would See Jesus
Finding in Jesus everything we need

OSWALD J SMITH
The Revival We Need
A heart-stirring cry for revival
The Enduement of Power
The power of the Holy Spirit in the Christian life

CHARLES FINNEY
Revival
God's way of revival

Please ask for these titles at your local
Christian bookshop

RHP One Pound Classics

Revival

by Charles Finney

"Wilt thou not revive us again: that thy people may rejoice in thee?"

Charles Finney's writings on revival have led the way to genuine revival time and time again. The spiritual truths that have had such an impact on past generations remain the same today, and Finney shows how the heavens can open and revival can come whenever people are willing to count the cost.

"In this book an attempt has been made to gather the main points from the large amount of material available, in order to provide a handbook for those Christian workers who would learn the simple principles which govern the promise of Revival.

"It is taken for granted that God's blessing will come in His own way and in His own good time, but Finney shows that the scriptures have made it plain that blessing follows when certain conditions are fulfilled in the hearts and lives of men." — E.E. SHELHAMER

Now available from your local Christian bookshop